A Theology of Japan Monograph Series Vol. 9

Raising Leaders through Sufferings beyond Walls

A Theology of Japan
Monograph Series ❾

Edited by Atsuyoshi Fujiwara and Brian Byrd

Raising Leaders through Sufferings beyond Walls

Centurial Vision for Post-disaster Japan

The Great East Japan Earthquake International Theological Symposium 3

Juan Martínez
David Boan
George Kalantzis
Brian Byrd

 SEIGAKUIN UNIVERSITY PRESS

"A Theology of Japan" Monograph Series

Editorial Board:
Mitsuharu Akudo
Yoshibumi Takahashi
Atsuyoshi Fujiwara
Brian Byrd

All rights reserved. No part of this publication may be reproduced, stored in retrieval system, or transmitted in any form or by any means, electronic, mechanical, photocopying, recording, or otherwise without the prior permission of the publisher.

©2016 Seigakuin University General Research Institute

"A Theology of Japan" Monograph Series
Vol. 9 Raising Leaders through Sufferings beyond Walls:
Centurial Vision for Post-disaster Japan
Published by
Seigakuin University Press
1-1 Tosaki, Ageo-shi, Saitama
Japan 362-8585
press@seigakuin-univ.ac.jp

ISBN978-4-907113-16-2 C3316

To Professor Glen Herald Stassen

After the editing of the previous volume, I received the news of Professor Glen Stassen's death. We are so grateful for his visit to Japan for the first theological symposium in 2012. The stimulating, thought-provoking conversations Glen, I and other friends enjoyed during his visit remain fresh in my mind. Before the symposium, we had the opportunity to travel together to hard-hit coastal communities and see the devastation of the earthquake and tsunami. Along the way, we met with victims of the disaster and people working for relief and restoration, and paused each time to listen to stories and join in prayer. At the symposium, Glen spoke to us from the Gospel of Mark on the cross as compassionate suffering and confrontation of injustice. He also offered his personal apologies for the atomic bombs dropped on Hiroshima and Nagasaki. This disaster moved Glen, then a young boy, to dedicate his life to peacemaking. Glen touched the hearts of many here with this message, and with his sensitivity, openness, and wisdom.

We thus dedicate this issue to Glen, teacher and practitioner of just peacemaking, who sought to walk in the way of Jesus through suffering and beyond.

Atsuyoshi Fujiwara

Preface

Preface

We held the Third Great East Japan Earthquake International Theological Symposium with Fuller Theological Seminary on February 15 and 17, 2014 at Ochanomizu Christian Center in Tokyo. This is a report from the symposium. We were pleased that an extension of the symposium took place in Kobe on February 13, 2014 at Aotani Evangelical Lutheran Church, supported by three seminaries (Kobe Lutheran Theological Seminary, Kansai Bible College and Evangelical Biblical Seminary). Kobe is the city that suffered a major earthquake in 1995. We were also delighted to have two professors from Wheaton College joining the symposium as speakers.

The theme of the first symposium was "How Can We Start Again? Centurial Vision for Post-disaster Japan." This became the overarching theme for the three yearly symposiums. The second symposium's theme was "The Church: Embracing the Sufferers, Moving Forward." One of the strengths of the symposiums was our network with the local working groups, through which we were able to see the reality on the ground. With this perspective, we could discuss and prepare symposium themes useful for the church in Japanese society. We chose "Raising Leaders through Sufferings beyond Walls" as the theme of the third symposium. When you look ahead to the future, to 100 years from today, raising and training young Christian leaders is an urgent and essential challenge. We contacted KGK (Kirisutosha Gakusei Kai, the Japanese affiliate of the International Fellowship of Evangelical Students) and SCF (Student Christian Fellowship) of the United Church of Christ in Japan, along with seminaries and Christian universities. We hoped that young Christians and seekers could have opportunities to meet together in various ways through, before, and after the symposium. Unlike the first and second symposiums where we met just for one day, we added a second day especially for young people at the third symposium.

We started the Great East Japan Earthquake International Theological Symposium with two purposes. One was to encourage theological discussion in plain language regarding the disaster for the church and ordinary believers. Everyone was seeking some kind of answer and a space for theological dialogue after the massive disaster. The other was to develop personal relationships amongst Christian leaders beyond denominational and other unnecessary walls. We intentionally provided several opportunities throughout the year to have face-to-face dialogue as we prepared for the next symposium. We were pleased to have participants not only from mainline denominations and evangelical churches, but for the last two years from the Roman Catholic Church as well. After all, the Christian population is less than 1% in this country. And more importantly, Christ calls us to serve one another and the world as one body. We should work together wherever we can.

Over the past three years we were able to create an "open space" for people to meet, share their stories, gain new insights, and partner together for the work of the gospel in Japan. We plan to continue this into the future.

Revd. Atsuyoshi Fujiwara, Ph.D.

Chair, The Great East Japan Earthquake International Symposium Committee
Professor, School of Global Studies and Collaboration, Aoyama Gakuin Univ.

A Theology of Japan Monograph Series Vol. 9
Raising Leaders through Sufferings beyond Walls

Contents

Preface   Atsuyoshi Fujiwara   9

Part I

Lecture 1

Suffering and Serving in the Way of Jesus:

     Meaning Making in Response to Disaster   Juan Martínez   15

Panel Discussion

The Practice of Social Welfare Built on an Understanding of Relationships

Yoshito Inamatsu   29

The Work of Caritas   Isao Kikuchi   36

Holistic Gospel Ministry   Masanori Kurasawa   43

The Japan Baptist Convention and the Great East Japan Earthquake

     and Tsunami Disaster   Michio Hamano   48

Workshop Report

Workshop 1: Considerations in Psychological Counseling

Creating New Narratives and Rituals   Akira Fujikake   57

Care for Stress of the Heart and Soul   Hajime Hori   60

Workshop 2: Support and Ministry

The Dilemma of Mission in Tohoku:

Balancing Physical Relief and Spiritual Salvation Makoto Suzuki 63

Miyagi Mission Network Yukikazu Otomo 67

Workshop 3: Rituals

How to Engage with Rites for the Dead and Traditional Folkways

  Takashi Yoshida 71

Plenary Session

What Disasters Teach the Church David Boan 75

Lecture 2

'Whose Feet Are You Washing?' Raising Leaders in the Midst of Suffering

  George Kalantzis 94

Part II

Christian Forum for Reconciliation in Northeast Asia:

 A New Community of Friendship Brian Byrd 103

Contributors

About the Authors 123

Part I

Lecture 1
Suffering and Serving in the Way of Jesus:
Meaning Making in Response to Disaster

Juan Martínez

Three years have now passed since the March 11, 2011 disaster. The cycle of three annual symposiums that were born out of the disaster is being completed with this event. It was a pleasure to be with you during the first symposium and I am happy to be with you again as we complete this cycle of reflections on this event and its aftermath.

I wish to begin by naming the importance of the fact that you all are here together today. Japanese Christians have responded to this disaster in ways that are unprecedented in modern Japanese Christian history. This three year cycle of symposiums have given testimony to the fact that Christians across many theological traditions are thinking together about what it means to be a Christian in Japan today and about your role in Japanese society together. That is very good news, in and of itself.

When one is in the midst of a disaster, particularly one of massive proportions, one usually focuses on the uniqueness of one's experience. In many ways each situation, each disaster is unique. The March 11th disaster created a unique situation for Japan and for the Christian Church in this country. But over time it becomes important to both recognize the uniqueness, but also the commonality to the human experience of all disasters. All suffering is unique and individual, but suffering is common to all humanity. It is because of the commonness that we can talk to each about our suffering and the reason that we can learn from each other. That is why it is particularly important that you begin to tell and re-tell your experiences. In that process you will connect with each other, but will also be able to connect with others who have lived through disasters and have learned to connect their experiences with the flow of God's redemption in human history. Narrative and reinterpretation allows us to provide marco meaning to our unique experience.

As time passes our perspective changes, which then affects how we interpret formative events like these. By choosing to focus on re-telling the stories during this third symposium you are recognizing that we humans do in fact return to key events in our histories and re-interpret them for our new situations. Our Christian Scriptures provide an obvious model. Particularly in the Old Testament Israel regularly retells and re-interprets the core formational narratives of the call of Abraham, the Exodus and the Exile. This is done in light of new circumtances that call Israel to re-imagine what God has done in the past as a way of making sense of the present. In Scripture this process connects the present situation to what we confess about God's previous interventions. This provides hope that the present situation will someday also be seen in a similar light. It gives us a framework to interpret the present situation. But it also invites us to believe that God will be, and is, present as we recover and look toward a new future.

So now, three years after March 11, it is time to recount the disaster and to re-tell the stories specifically of how Christians responded to the situation. This will mean re-visiting the pain, but also the courage, the commitment and the sacrifice. But the principal reason this process will be important is that you will re-tell the story in light of God's presence. It will be then that the suffering can be given a framing within God's work in the world and that you will be better ready to serve others in the name of Christ because of your own painful experience.

My small contribution to this process today will be to invite you to re-examine the events through the lenses of God's lived presence in the midst of your suffering. I was not here, I am not Japanese and I have never lived through a disaster of this magnitude. So the best I can do is point to the experiences of others and invite us to learn together.

In events such as the March 11, 2011 disaster humans suffer profoundly, but others also have the opportunity of serving those who are suffering. As followers of Jesus Christ we recognize that these two actions, suffering and service, come together in the person of Christ. But they also must be linked in our work in the name of Christ.

Today I want us to think about the link between suffering and service in the way of Jesus, then about some of the theological lessons we can learn from suffering, and lastly talk about why telling the stories is so important for the recovery process. Because I am an Anabaptist I will draw from this tradition and frame the issues from that perspective. Of course, I recognize that Anabaptism as ideal and Anabaptism as practiced faith do not always match up. We are just as fallen as other Christians, but our theology invites us to take the intersection of suffering and service seriously. So I hope that an Anabaptist reading will be helpful as you re-examine where you have been and where you are going. (And for those of you who are not Anabaptists, I invite you to draw on those places in your own theological traditions where you can make these types of connections.) But I will also draw from Henri Nouwen and the way he invites us to take seriously the importance of re-remembering as we find meaning and hope in the midst of disaster.

Discipleship: Suffering and Serving in the Way of Jesus

There is probably no better concise summary of the Anabaptist understanding of the link between suffering, service, and the way of Jesus than the words of Menno Simons, the converted 16th century Dutch priest who became our namesake, first as a mark of derision and then as an example of commitment. (Of course, it also helps that Menno was one of the few leaders of the first generation that was not martyred and who lived long enough to have his name used as an accusatory nickname for the Anabaptist communities he led and served.)

True evangelical faith is of such a nature it cannot lie dormant; but manifests itself out in all righteousness and works of love; it dies unto flesh and blood; destroys forbidden lusts and desires; cordially seeks, serves and fears God; clothes the naked; feeds the hungry; consoles the afflicted; shelters the destitute; aids and consoles all the oppressed; returns good for evil; serves those that injure it; prays for those that persecute it; teaches, admonishes and reproves with the Word of the Lord; seeks that which is lost; binds up that which is wounded; heals the sick and saves that which is strong (sound); it becomes all things to all people. The persecution, suffering and anguish that come to it for the sake of the Lord's truth have become a glorious joy and comfort to it. [1]

This statement, which became somewhat of an anthem with the name "True Evangelical Faith" among many Mennonites, clearly connects transformation, service and suffering. While Roman Catholics and the magisterial Reformers were arguing about doctrinal or liturgical signs of the true church, the Anabaptists focused on the fruits of God's work in those who committed themselves to Jesus Christ. A key part of this statement is Menno's declaration that true faith "becomes all things to all people." From an Anabaptist perspective the most obvious sign of a true evangelical faith is to serve those in need, including the ones who seek your harm. In another occasion Menno also said:

Is it not sad and intolerable hypocrisy that these poor people boast of having the Word of God, of being the true Christian church, never remembering that they have entirely lost their sign of true Christianity? .... they suffer many of their own poor, afflicted members (notwithstanding their fellow believers have received one baptism and partaken of the same bread with them) to ask alms; and poor, hungry, suffering, old, lame, blind, and sick people to beg their bread at their doors. [2]

Because Anabaptism was born and shaped in suffering and persecution during the 16th century, members of the movement could not avoid addressing these issues and their practical implications from early on. Suffering became an important framer and theological marker for those who chose to follow Christ from an Anabaptist perspective. Several things stand out as they thought about suffering and about how to respond to it.

In the first place, suffering does not come as a surprise. Suffering is part of the human condition, but also something that can be expected by those who follow the way of Christ. If we are not ready to suffer we are not ready to live life

Suffering and Serving in the Way of Jesus

and certainly are not ready to follow Christ. This is not a fatalistic and inevitable perspective on suffering. But it is a confession that we live in a broken world, one where the good suffer, but also one where bad things happen to all.

There is a profound theology in this understanding. There is a time to ask complex and painful questions about the brokenness of creation and also about how evil functions in the world. But true faith starts from a commitment to respond to the need. Yet even as we seek to alleviate suffering, we also recognize that this side of Christ's reign, we can anticipate that suffering will continue, be it because of persecution, injustice, natural disasters, or the disasters humans create. We can, and must, work to create a better world, but our human efforts will not eliminate suffering.

But, secondly, suffering is also a key part of the redemptive work of Christ. Christ carries our pain as He redeems us. The cross is not only the means that God uses to bring us life, it is also the way of life of those who follow Christ. From an Anabaptist perspective one cannot understand what it means to follow Christ if we are not willing to suffer with Him and in His name. In Hans Denck's words: "No one can truly know unless he follow him in life, and no one may follow him unless he has first known him." [3]

While the magisterial reformers were debating about the signs of a true church among themselves, with Anabaptists and others, service and suffering became Anabaptist signs of a faithful church. This was not a doctrinal statement, but the lived experience of a movement, particularly during the first generations of the movement when thousands of Anabaptists were martyred for their faith.

Throughout the history of the church there have been people and movements that idealized or ritualized suffering, and Anabaptists have not been inmune to this tendency. But by joining service and suffering one avoids making suffering an end in itself, and this can help keep one focused on the fact that the cross is at the center of the way of Jesus. To this day, many Mennonite homes have a copy of the *Martyrs' Mirror*. (I have mine in my office.) This is a large book that includes the stories of martyrs throughout the history of the church, but includes a very large section of the Anabaptist martyrs of the early years of the movement. But one of the most important and retold stories is that of Dirk Willems.

Willems was a 16th century Anabaptist who had been jailed for his faith. He was able to escape from incarceration and flee. While being chased by his jailer Willems began to run across a frozen pond. Because the persecutor was heavier than he, the persecutor broke through the ice and was in danger of losing his life. Willems turned back and saved the man, who then arrested him and took him back to jail and to later face martyrdom.

Martyrs' Mirror, and this story in particular, are important as a herme-neutical key. Telling and re-telling this type of story is an invitation to return to formative experiences that helped define and frame this expression of the faith. The important thing for us today is that we can better understand what it means to follow Christ when we re-tell the stories of suffering and service of those who have chosen to follow Christ despite the cost. This re-telling calls us to remember the cost of faithfulness, but it also a call to connect our own experiences to the importance of being faithful today.

Thirdly, if the way of Christ is the way of the cross, then the intersection of suffering and service is an important place where we can find God's presence in our lives. God works in the midst of our suffering and invites us to recognize His work even in places of pain. That is always easier said than done, particularly when the suffering is overwhelming.

Anabaptists did not focus their energy talking about the injustice or unjust suffering, particularly against themselves, though they did question the ways of war of the day and declared that the persecution they were suffering was wrong. They accepted that suffering was part of being followers of Jesus Christ. What was most important to them was how a Christian was to respond. If one saw need one was to respond, whether or not they were Christians, no matter the reason, nor the potential consequences.

But among the Anabaptists suffering was not only what one person experienced, it was the common experience of the community. They found meaning in

Suffering and Serving in the Way of Jesus

the experience as they told and re-told the testimonies of suffering, and service, for the cause of Christ. As they read Scripture in light of their suffering they were able to understand that they stood in historical continuity with those who had suffered before them in the name of Christ. By re-telling the various stories they were able to reaffirm their faith and to give meaning to their suffering. It was a community experience that had meaning because it was like the suffering of Jesus. They were suffering and serving in the way of Jesus.

In his *The Theology of Anabaptism* Robert Friedmann argues that the 16th century movement did not, and could not, have an explicit theological system.[4] He argues that they had an existential Christian expression in which life and faith were closely connected. They were not nearly as concerned about the exact doctrinal debates of the Reformers and the Roman Catholics. They were committed to living out the way of Jesus. One of those ways that they knew they were following Jesus was in how they responded to the needs of others. The commitment to following Jesus meant that they would respond to the suffering of others, whether friend or persecutor, whether Anabaptist or not, or even if they were non-Christians.

This type of response was very concrete and demanded one use the resources God has given them.

> Each man should have regard for his neighbor, so that the hungry might be fed, the thirsty refreshed, the naked clothed. For we are not lords of our own property, but stewards and dispensers.[5]

In practice this became a threat to 16th century European society. Anabaptists saw that Christians had to use what they had to serve those in need. Some, like the Hutterites, decided to practice the full community of goods. But though most Anabaptists did not draw the same conclusion, all realized the importance of sharing and providing for all. In practice this meant that the community served as a type of mutual insurance. The loads of suffering would not be carried by one person or family on their own. Caring for the needs of others was not "merely" service, it was also a key means of witness. Also, a sign of true conversion was the willingness to serve others, no matter the cost.

Learning from Suffering

As Christians we confess that several types of suffering can be redemptive. Clearly our assumptions are based on our theology. We confess that God works in the world and that the focal point of God's work is the person and work of Jesus Christ. Since we recognize that Christ did His work through suffering on the cross, we confess that suffering that is linked to the cross and to the work God is doing in the world is clearly redemptive. But we also recognize that a lot of human suffering does not easily fit into that category. Nonetheless, as Christians we also confess that God can redeem all human suffering, even when it is clearly unjust, unfair or uncontrolable. I would like to suggest some of the ways that suffering can be redemptive.

1. Suffering that is done for the cause of Christ
2. Suffering done in the service of others in the name of Christ
3. Suffering that is connected to the suffering of Christ
4. When we allow God to use suffering in our lives to transform us into the image of Christ
5. When we walk through it in the hope of God's presence and hope of the resurrection

The problem in practice is that some types of suffering more easily fit into one of these categories than others. But another important issue is interpretative. How do we understand the role and reality of suffering in human experience? As we walk through each of these "confessions" we recognize that they connect in different ways to our understanding of what it means to follow Jesus and how we understand the human experience.

Most Christian traditions have their martyr stories, the testimonies by or about those who suffered for their faith. The number of people around the world who suffer or who have died for being Christians continues to be high in many parts of the world. We would very likely name that as redemptive suffering. Anabaptists would say that if you do not suffer you need to ask whether you have a clear and consistent Christian witness.

Suffering and Serving in the Way of Jesus

Related to this is the suffering or death of those who give Christian witness or put themselves in harm's way to serve the cause of Christ. We raise these type of people as examples (though many of us are not as sure that we want to suffer martyrdom). But suffering can also be making a sacrifice to serve those in need, specifically those that are suffering. When Christians choose to give their life to mission and service, this can be understood as a type of suffering, in that they are making a type of sacrifice. This is a form of being Christ for the other, giving not from what is left over, but from the center of my being and existence in the name of Christ.

But our task also has to be helping people redeem the suffering that they experience. Because of the various ways that we interpret our world, suffering can quickly be fatalistic or "meaningless" when it either becomes an end in and of itself or when there is no interpretative framing to the experience. As you begin the task of telling and re-telling the stories of the disaster and the responses to it, you have the opportunity of helping people tell their experiences in ways that provide meaning to their suffering. Part of that meaning making process will call us to allow God to work in our lives and also to walk in the hope of His presence and His future. We do that is by connecting our stories with God's grand narrative and work in human history.

Telling Stories of Suffering

In his book *The Living Reminder* Henry Nouwen talks about the pastoral importance of helping people remember and re-tell their experiences, particularly of pain, sin and suffering. According to Nouwen the task of the minister is to be a healing, sustaining and guiding reminder, walking with people as they re-tell their stories. Each one of these aspects provide important framings for helping us address our experiences of suffering and pain.

The events of our lives are probably less important than the form they take in the totality of our story. Different people remember a similar illness, accident, succes, or surprise in very different ways, and much of their sense of self derives less from what happened than from how they remember what

23

happened, how they have placed the past events into their own personal history. [6]

According to Nouwen one of the most frequent pastoral encounters is a "suffering of memories." Those memories wound us because when we have experienced pain or suffering we try to forget or to bury them. Our pastoral task is not to take the pain away, but to connect it to the greater sorrow, that suffered by our Lord.

By connecting the human story with the story of the suffering servant, we rescue our history from its fatalistic chain and allow our time to be converted from chronos into kairos, from a series of randomly organized incidents and accidents into a constant opportunity to explore God's work in our lives. [7]

As we learn to connect our suffering to the suffering of Christ we are invited to recognize that we are sustained in this life by His work and the promise of His presence. But we learn about his presence even as we live today in his absence and the promise of the presence of the Holy Spirit. So in the "midst of pains and tribulations the first sign of the new life can be found and a joy can be experienced which is hidden in the midst of sadness." [8] In the act of remembering we can begin to experience the new life of the Spirit and the fact that God continues to sustain us. But it also reminds us that God continues to do new things and can guide us toward a renewed future.

Nouwen says that "good memories offer good guidance" because our hopes are built on memories. In particular, it is the memory of Jesus that gives "hope and confidence in the midst of a failing culture, a faltering society, and a dark world." [9] And we could add, as we face the pain of disaster.

As we re-tell the stories that guide us pastoral leaders need to do two important things. On the one hand, there will be a need to help people recognize the temptation to think that what they did was a "perfect" practice of the faith, that what Japanese Christians did in response to the March 11 was the church at its best. On the other hand, it will be important to focus on those stories that best embody the vision, practices that point to the call of Jesus to suffer and serve in

24

Suffering and Serving in the Way of Jesus

His name. As we create this process of remembering and re-telling we serve as God's ministers in the midst of suffering.

Moving Forward

As you begin to gain the perspective of time in relationship to the March 11 disaster, it is a good moment for you to begin to collect your stories, your testimonies of what happened and how God was present in the midst of the suffering and service. I come from a specific Latino church tradition where telling testimonies was an important part of how we confessed our faith, how we worshipped, and how we recognized God's work in our lives. These were opportunities to rehearse our faith and its connection to our daily lives. But it was also a moment to provide support to others. The message we gave to each other and to those from outside who were listening was: "If God is working here, God can also work in your circumstances."

That is why the task on which you are embarking is so crucial. Of course, you will need to talk about the pain and the loss. Part of re-telling the story of disaster is to continue the grieving process. Linked to that, the Japanese people, and the Christian community in particular, will need to confess that things were not as you thought they were and that no matter how much we plan we cannot control our own future. In a sense, one of the reasons we need to re-tell the stories is that we need to face our limitations and confess our need of God.

But you will also tell the testimonies of service and of sacrifice. You have many stories to share about how people responded to the needs of others, often risking, or losing, their own lives, to make it possible for others to live. With that will come the powerful testimonies of conversion and encounter, where people found God in the midst of this disaster. Throughout Japan, and particularly in the affected areas, there are people around you who encountered Jesus Christ in the midst of the suffering and/or through the witness of those who responded to the need. We need to tell those stories of how God transformed disaster into light for many and also encouraged many Christians to re-affirm their faith and witness.

The March 11 disaster and its aftermath also brought people who worked side by side. Be it the volunteers from around the world, Christians and non-Christians, be it the inter-religious response, or "merely" the neighbor who provided a glass of water, there will be many stories about how people worked together to serve those in need. As these stories are told they will also reflect how people learned about each other and how they grew in commitments to serve others across the differences that defined them. In particular, Christians will have stories about how they learned to relate to other Christians about how they caught a new vision of the place of Christians in Japanese society.

There is an interesting sense in which the tsunami not only broke down seawalls. Your responses are testimony to how this disaster also served to break down the walls that have existed between Japanese Christians of various denominations and also between Christians and larger Japanese society. Something is at work and you may only be able to give initial testimony to it. It may be years down the line before you are able to more clearly describe how old walls were broken and new relationships and missional commitments were developed.

But the stories will also invite us to recognize the human role in the long term impact of the disaster. Sharing narratives about March 11 has to also look at the complex issues of how part of the disaster is directly related to human responsibility to creation care. How did Christians respond to this larger issue and how does this disaster invite a new narrative and conversation about God's call to humans to be stewards of creation?

But the stories will also have to address the issue of our mortality. To face disaster is to recognize that we will all die, be it in the middle of a disaster, because of illness, or "merely" of old age. But expressing our mortality will also invite us to proclaim that we believe "in the resurrection of the body and life everlasting."

Sharing what has happened will also help people think about the work still pending. How can the church in Japan become a better servant of Japanese society? How can the churches in Japan work better together to give clear Christian witness? How and where do we see God at work in the midst of the disaster and its aftermath? How does Japanese society need to think differently about itself in light of March 11, and what role can Christians play in working through that process? These types of questions will give the stories a future oriented focus which God can use to guide the Christian churches of Japan toward a more faithful commitment to God's mission in this country.

In this process we connect our stories and the stories of those who suffered, of those who served, and of those who suffered and served, into the service and suffering of Jesus Christ and of God's work in the world. Those stories are connected to the stories of believers around the world and throughout the centuries. And so we continue to walk together in the way of Christ.

1) In "The Reasons Why Menno Simon Does Not Cease Teaching and Writing" published in *The Complete Works of Menno Simon*, Aylmer, Ontario and Lagrange, Indiana: Pathway Publishers, 1983, 246.

2) From "True Christian Faith" quoted in *Anabaptism in Outline*, Walter Klaassen, editor. Kitchener, Ontario & Scottdale, Pennsylvania: Herald Press, 1981, 241.

3) From "The Contention that Scripture Says" in *Anabaptism*, 87.

4) See *The Theology of Anabaptism* by Robert Friedmann, Kitchener, Ontario & Scottdale, Pennsylvania: Herald Press, 1973, particularly 27–34.

5) Quote from Balthaser Hubmaier in "Conversation on Zwingli's Book on Baptism" in *Anabaptism*, 233.

6) Henri Nouwen, *The Living Reminder: Service and Prayer in Memory of Jesus Christ*, New York: Harper San Francisco, 2009, 19.

7) Ibid, 25.

8) Ibid, 47.

9) Ibid, 59, 62.

Panel Discussion
The Practice of Social Welfare Built on an Understanding of Relationships

Yoshito Inamatsu

After this the Lord appointed seventy-two others and sent them two by two ahead of him to every town and place where he was about to go. He told them, "The harvest is plentiful, but the workers are few. Ask the Lord of the harvest, therefore, to send out workers into his harvest field. Go! I am sending you out like lambs among wolves. Do not take a purse or bag or sandals; and do not greet anyone on the road. When you enter a house, first say, 'Peace to this house.' If someone who promotes peace is there, your peace will rest on them; if not, it will return to you. Stay there, eating and drinking whatever they give you, for the worker deserves his wages. Do not move around from house to house. When you enter a town and are welcomed, eat what is offered to you. Heal the sick who are there and tell them, 'The kingdom of God has come near to you.'"

Luke 10:1–9, NIV

Introduction

I was raised in a Christian home, studied social welfare at a Christian-founded school, and immediately upon my graduation thirty-five years ago this spring, I went to work for a Christian social welfare institution. Within Japanese society, I have lived and worked in a relatively Christian environment, but I am a layperson, not a pastor or theologian. I cannot say I have the credentials needed to address this international theological symposium. Nevertheless, as I have done before in similar situations, I would be happy if summarizing my thoughts on what I have experienced and felt in the contexts and roles to which I have been assigned would be of some use to you.

The Great Earthquake

The Great East Japan Earthquake Disaster has forced me to reflect deeply on the practice of social welfare in which we have been involved up to now. When the earthquake struck at 2:46 pm on March 11, 2011, the Japan Christian Social Work League happened to be holding a board meeting in a hotel opposite the train station in Hamamatsu, Shizuoka Prefecture. We had finished with our agenda and were preparing to adjourn when we felt a slow but long-lasting horizontal rolling motion. We had yet to grasp the magnitude of the quake, so we finished the meeting, and I returned to my work at the institution that I direct in Hamamatsu near the coast. There, I saw the spine-chilling televised coverage of the tsunami and learned of the tsunami warning in effect for the Shizuoka coastline as well.

After directing my institution to make appropriate emergency preparations, I tried to find out what I could about the situation in our related institutions in the Tohoku area. I had great difficulty in making connections, but finally after two or three days I could confirm that these institutions were still in operation. I contacted the other board members, and we decided to send workers, should they be requested by institutions in the disaster area. We continued in our efforts to gather information. In fact, however, we had no requests to send workers. The disaster area was too far away, too cut off, and covered too wide of an area for us to take clear action on our own. We found ourselves in the dilemma of thinking that we had to do something in this situation, yet realizing that our ill-prepared actions could actually add to the burden of those in the disaster area.

Our association is made up of social welfare institutions related to the United Church of Christ in Japan (Nihon Kirisuto Kyodan). In April, the Kyodan set up a committee to deal with the disaster, with one representative on the committee to be from our association. From May, I took on this responsibility and began attending meetings of the Kyodan Great East Japan Disaster Relief Planning Headquarters Committee. In the meetings, I felt the weakness of an organization made up of churches with a variety of backgrounds in making decisions quickly and taking action. This was no different from what I felt regarding the capacity of our own association to respond quickly to needs.

30

Looking back now, I feel that our social welfare association took the same course as the Kyodan committee, debating matters such as support for the affected churches and local disaster victims. Putting aside consideration of how effective we might have been, we did our best in each group to cover the ground we could. Even if the members of our organization could not all function together, we did manage to take small actions like sending care workers to one affected region.

Christian Social Work in Japan

Missionaries from overseas founded many of the historic Christian social welfare institutions in Japan. Individual Japanese Christian benefactors through their strong leadership founded others. Missionaries left their home countries and made their homes in Japanese society, rooting themselves and sharing the gospel in local communities, and engaging in social welfare ministry to those excluded from society. Unable to overlook the misery of those on the fringes of society, Japanese Christian benefactors began what would later become institutions by welcoming needy people into their own homes or on their property, sharing daily life together with them.

Many of those around supported this charity work of missionaries and Japanese benefactors, but there were indeed few instances in which the church in Japan saw such work as their calling and engaged in it as an organization over the long term. There were also many social welfare institutions that grew out of the prayers of a church, where the church then assumed responsibility for running the institution. However, as these institutions have become part of the public system and dependent on public funding, and as the percentage of non-Christian workers in these institutions has increased, I sense that the connection between institutions and churches has become rather weak.

Inward–looking Churches and Business-oriented Social Welfare Organizations

Through our involvement with relief efforts during this disaster, I sensed that both churches and institutions share weak points. Of course, this is not true of all churches, and it is not as though no social welfare organizations took initiative in offering aid in the affected areas. On the whole, however, I believe this weakness was present. As one both raised within the church and involved in social welfare, I do feel the need in some areas for reflection on the way we have acted up to now.

In the Bible passage I read today, the Lord Jesus sends workers out into the towns and villages to live together with the people there, praying for the peace of each house that they relate with, and proclaiming the coming near of the kingdom of God.

The gospel of Christ is not only proclaimed to and for those who are gathered in the church. It must also be proclaimed to those in the towns and villages, those living in areas outside of the church. Missionaries from overseas and church planting pastors went out and established churches. However, is it not the case that those of us now gathered in these churches remain inside, with no intention of going outside to continue the work of the gospel?

Christian benefactors opened up their own lives and established communities for social welfare. These communities were eventually recognized as institutions within the government system that developed. There, within the system, they achieved financial stability. We came to work within this framework of stability, maintaining separately our own residences, relying on the support provided only within this closed system. Institutions, although located in a community, have become walled off from the community, where social welfare is understood as only that which is practiced within the institution.

Therefore, as in this case where an emergency arises at a place located away from our daily lives, it does become a bit easier for disaster victims to be received within institutions. However, many conditions force an institution to hesitate from discontinuing its normal operations and going outside to work. Even if a worker is sent out, I am afraid that person experiences no little confusion in trying to work and make decisions outside of the usual framework.

The People to Whom We Relate

In doing the work of social welfare, it is hardly unusual to encounter people isolated within society. We also hear so often through the mass media of social welfare issues such as bullying, abuse, domestic violence, poverty, suicide, and crime. I think that those living in troubled environments, even without facing the

The Practice of Social Welfare Built on an Understanding of Relationships

shock of the earthquake and disaster, lose their dignity and are forced to suffer social isolation, full of distress and sorrow. Even though we know these things, if we choose not to become involved, are we not just like those caught on video standing still, unable to take a single step in the face of the oncoming tsunami? And with the passage of one year, two years, we have likely forgotten that time, and the dilemma in which we felt our hearts so intensely shaken and moved.

My Experience at Kohitsujigakuen (Lambs' School)

In my work at Kohitsujigakuen, I have met and shared daily life with severely handicapped children. In the past, these children were excluded from the education system, and unable to communicate even their own needs. They could not function without many kinds of care. Among them were children whose different sense of reality made it impossible for them to adapt to their environment, and who exhibited severe behavioral disorders.

When working with disturbed children, the staff feel so painfully their lack of power, and that their heart might break due to their inability to communicate with the children. They wanted to ask as in the Bible, "Why did God give them a life such as this?" Often we wanted to question again the teaching of Jesus: "How are we to see the glory of God in the life of this child?" Was it enough just to provide them with food and a place to live, and to care for their bodily needs? We would feel no joy, I thought, if we suppressed our personal emotions and just went through the motions in our work each day, telling ourselves to expect no more.

Day in and day out, however, we have to wrestle bodily and head on with the intense, wordless cries of children regarding their lives, and strive to discern what they are seeking and what they are trying to communicate. In this struggle, we come to appreciate each person there as being absolutely necessary, as having ultimate worth.

When we relate with these absolutely necessary people of ultimate worth, no matter what disability of difficulties they may face, we do not think of these disabilities or difficulties as making them of no worth. Knowing these people as ones of ultimate worth, caregivers realize that they and those they work with have been given a place to live. Caregivers, in personal relations with others, have come to feel value and purpose in the work of social welfare.

Living in Relationships

In the earthquake disaster, support for people that lost family members, livelihoods, and hope for the future cannot stop merely at providing material support, or guaranteeing living expenses. Looking to the future, the question must be asked, "How we can live with hope?"

Three years ago, when the Great East Japan Earthquake placed us in a state of emergency, not only the victims, but also many people not directly affected by the disaster sought for a kind of "bonding," or relationships. Also, even though in a state of emergency, seeing Japanese people caring for their relationships with others led to praise from observers overseas. Maybe we unconsciously realized that it is truly as we live in relationships with others that we have hope for living.

However, as three years have passed from that time of crisis, and rebuilding has gradually progressed—this certainly a reason for rejoicing—we have sought to guarantee our lives by visible things of material value and through material things to confirm our own value in living.

Social Welfare Founded on the Gospel of Christ

The Bible teaches us to pray "Peace on this house," eating the food served and sharing life together with those in the house. We discover true peace in the midst of the relationships God has given us, and demonstrate this peace in our forgiving each other and in regarding each other as important. Is it not the case that when we sense this sort of peace we can declare, "the kingdom of God has come near to you?" The basis of our practical service is not the kind of support we give to those in trouble, or how much we can ensure provision of their needs for daily life. Rather, it is in continuing to relate to each person as important. Certainly, we feel painfully our powerlessness as we relate closely to those who have lost irreplaceable people in their lives, or their livelihood. All we can do is to come alongside them. However, even though we do not have sufficient power, if Christ is there with us, we surely can feel the salvation of God in that relationship. It is indeed in this relationship with God, in the cross and resurrection of Christ that we discover our true place of peace and rest, and the gift of eternal life that goes beyond our lives in this world.

The Practice of Social Welfare Built on an Understanding of Relationships

No matter what our challenging situation may entail, as we puzzle over what it means to be given life, and tell of the hope we discover in knowing life that we cannot lose, lived out in precious relationships with others, is this not the practice of social welfare rooted in the gospel of Christ? I fervently hope that social welfare established on and practiced in this rock-solid understanding of relationships develop in our walk with those we have met though this earthquake disaster, in relation with those even now facing hardships in the disaster-struck areas. What a blessing it will be when churches make this happen, going out into the areas in which they have been established, proclaiming the gospel, bearing together the suffering of the people living there, doing holistically the work of social welfare.

(translated by Brian Byrd)

Panel Discussion
The Work of Caritas

Isao Kikuchi

Tohoku is my *furusato*, the place I came from. I was born in Miyako City in Iwate Prefecture and spent most of my early days in Morioka, the capital of Iwate. The Great Tohoku Earthquake and Tsunami in 2011 thus has for me a deeply personal meaning. The disaster changed the landscape of my *furusato* and took away from many of my old friends the ordinary lives they had enjoyed.

At this moment, I am president of both Caritas Japan and Caritas Asia. Caritas Internationalis, established in 1951, is a humanitarian assistance organization of the Catholic Church headquartered in the Vatican. It has more than 160 member organizations around the world, including twenty-three in Asia. Caritas has General Consultative Status in the Economic and Social Council of the United Nations.

The Catholic Bishops' Conference of Japan established Caritas Japan in 1970 as part of the Commission for Social Concern. Its mission is to organize domestic and international aid for development and disaster relief, oversee the Lenten collection and other collections, and promote awareness of social welfare activities.

What I Saw in My Hometown after the Disaster

Immediately after the disaster, a number of Caritas organizations in other countries began offering their assistance. We organized a teleconference to coordinate the Caritas response. But in order to make an efficient plan for the relief activities of the Catholic Church, we needed to visit the disaster area and meet Bishop Hiraga of Sendai. Major roads to Sendai were closed, and there was a shortage of fuel. On March 16, five days after the disaster, Bishop Tani, then

36

The Work of Caritas

Bishop of Saitama, two staff members of Caritas Japan and I managed to make our way through Yamagata City to Sendai. Bishop Hiraga and Father Komatsu, chancellor of the diocese, met us at Sendai Cathedral, where we discussed a plan for immediate relief activities.

For the next month, we were busy coordinating volunteers from all over Japan. In April, however, I finally found time to travel to Miyako, located much farther to the north. One of my childhood friends now directs the Catholic kindergarten there. She took me to Taro, a district of Miyako that had been surrounded by high-rise concrete barriers. These protective, castle-like walls once renowned as able to withstand a tsunami had fallen, swept away by the tsunami. I could not believe my eyes when I saw the concrete barriers of Taro completely destroyed, its pieces washed into the waters of the fishing port. The tsunami had washed away my friend's family home as well. Fortunately, her family members were all safe.

Then we climbed a hill overlooking the town and port. From the top of the hill, we could see on the other side of the town "San-no-iwa," a rock wall in the sea that stood fifty meters high. When my friend saw how the tsunami had completely destroyed the concrete barriers, she was sure that this rock wall had met the same fate. A few days later, however, she learned that the rock remained intact. What a difference between a man-made and a natural wall! Human technology and wisdom, compared to God's creative power and mystery, are so weak, so small, so meaningless.

Through our experiences of the disaster, including the accidents at the Fukushima Nuclear Power Plant, where uncertainty still prevails after three years, we found out that we had been made to believe with a false sense of confidence in our human abilities. It was just a dream. Also many of us found out we had lost the sense of transcendence, or of a God who is far bigger than human beings. This would be the result of secularization. We thought that human beings were able to control everything in this world with our technology. God was no more needed. "Pride leads to destruction, and arrogance to downfall" (Proverbs 16:18). This disaster has warned each of us to be humble enough to examine our lifestyle and change our attitude from self-pride to humility and obedience before the power of God.

Moreover, we found out through the disaster what had become the real priority for Japanese society: we had made such an enormous sacrifice for development. Now, it seems to me, the people of Japan have started to forget what we had realized after the disaster and are returning to the lifestyle they had before the disaster. We want to just forget about negative things and go back to enjoying our life. Because we want to maintain our lifestyle and continue the type of development we have done for so many decades, we refuse to give priority to helping needy and rejected people.

My Experience in Development and Relief Assistance

I was a missionary in Ghana, West Africa, from 1986 to 1994. I was assigned to live in a village in the bush without electricity or water supply. In 1995, I started to work as a volunteer for Caritas Japan. My first assignment was to be a coordinator in a Rwandan refugee camp. Since then I have been working for Caritas Japan in different capacities, especially with foreign assistance or aid. In my daily experience in Ghana and in other encounters with people in need, the phrase "everybody seems to have forgotten us" has echoed in my heart. People in different countries with a common burden repeat this phrase. Although they desperately need assistance to sustain their daily lives, this assistance has been cut off. This reflects the reality that most international NGOs disappear from the field after six months of operation. This leaves deep disappointment and despair among the local people. Such people in need should not be left behind, feeling that they are forgotten.

In order to show our willingness to be with people in need, what shall we do? Of course, it is important to continue to spend time with them. Physical presence must be the priority. But this kind of physical presence itself is not the key to prove our willingness to be with people in need. The most important point is to create a change of heart among local people through our presence among them. Without this change of heart, we spend our time in vain.

No one questions that direct material assistance is important immediately after the disaster. But the effect of such assistance is limited and short-term. The number of those who can benefit is also limited.

By contrast, assistance that creates a change in the hearts of local people has long-term and wide-ranging effects. Such assistance together with change of hearts brings hope and courage for the future, so that people in anxiety and need might find their own way to go forward. Assistance from outside should change hearts of people in need so that they may be able to stand by themselves and decide to start to walk towards the future. Outsiders should walk alongside them.

So as we tell local people in need that we will never forget them, we are not by ourselves to plan long-term stays in the area, but must seek how we can establish relationships with local people so that they can find hope and courage for the future. If we are not able to do so, we, the outsiders, will just create despair among people when we depart, and leave the local people feeling that they have been forgotten.

We who come to the disaster-hit area to give assistance have to realize that we are outsiders. Local people must take the leading role in the rehabilitation and development of their community.

In these senses, I believe that one who commits oneself to the relief and rehabilitation operation after major disasters has to be an "animator" who creates a change of heart among local people.

The Response of the Catholic Church in Japan to the Great Tohoku Earthquake

As I have mentioned above, the Catholic Church in Japan on March 16, 2011 established the Sendai Diocese Support Center (SDSC) in Sendai Cathedral, as Sendai Diocese covers Aomori, Iwate, Miyagi and Fukushima Prefectures, the main areas hit by the disaster. Caritas Japan was responsible for supporting relief activities of the SDSC. Since the disaster, eight volunteer bases have been established in the coastal areas. The SDSC decided to use parish facilities in these areas for its volunteer bases. The Catholic Bishops' Conference of Japan (CBCJ) also established the Support Team for Rehabilitation in order to coordinate the relief and rehabilitation activities planned by each of the sixteen dioceses in Japan.

In the activities of these eight volunteer bases, coordination with the local Social Welfare Council (*Shakyo*) is important. At the beginning, the volunteers were sent to do work such as clearing debris and cleaning damaged houses under the supervision of the local Social Welfare Council. As time has passed, visiting temporary housing units and opening "community cafes" to help evacuees keep peace of heart and mind have become the main activities of the volunteers. Caritas Japan has been supporting all the activities of the eight volunteer bases with donations from Japan and overseas, and hopes to be able to continue to do so for at least four more years.

At the same time, with special funds from overseas Member Organizations, Caritas Japan has been assisting several local programs that have not been able to attract public funding support, such as funding for Summer Festival activities or furnishing temporary shop facilities, as the government provides only structures for temporary shops.

In order to provide such assistance, dialogue and discussion with local communities and temporary housing residents' associations are a must for NGOs. From the beginning of our activities, we did not outwardly display our Catholic identity or titles but used the name "Caritas Japan" alone. We did not want to arouse the suspicion of local residents and evacuees that our activities were a kind of proselytizing by Christians, who are still a small minority in Japan. Also, many people still remember AUM Shinrikyo's deadly gas attack in 1995, which causes them to think that religious groups are dangerous to the public safety.

The assistance of Caritas Japan is not meant for Catholic Church facilities, except for hospitals and schools, and such assistance is not limited to Catholic facilities. Caritas Japan does not consider religion in offering its support. At the same time, as I discuss below, we do not hide our Christian identity when we

The Work of Caritas

conduct relief and rehabilitation activities in the field.

Evangelization through Our Witness in Relief and Rehabilitation Work

In conclusion, let me share how we proclaim the gospel message through our activities.

As I have mentioned, our volunteers do not ostensibly exhibit their Catholic identity while they are in action. But this does not mean we are hiding our identity. First and foremost, these volunteer bases are almost all located within Catholic Church facilities, making it obvious that we are Christians.

Secondly, more than half of the volunteers who have joined our activities so far have been non-Christians, so it is not possible for them to proclaim the gospel message as such. However, one point has to be considered important. A high percentage of our non-Christian volunteers are repeaters, those who have joined our activities several times. Why do they become repeaters? While we have not done any organized research, reports from the staff members of these volunteer bases suggest the answer to this question.

In the first year of activities, religious sisters (nuns) from all over Japan were sent to stay in the volunteer bases to take care of household duties such as providing meals. Sisters took turns, staying for a week and then handing over their work to the next group of sisters. We called this our "sisters relay." The sisters created a religious atmosphere in the bases as they made time for prayer and sharing of experiences each evening. No one was forced to join in these activities and yet many volunteers, including non-Christians, found meaning here. They found peace for their minds and hearts in these daily "spiritual" times, the main reason why non-Christian volunteers became repeaters. I believe this to be a perfect example of evangelization through the witness of faith. Without speaking directly about Christianity, Christians in the volunteer centers become living witnesses of the Word of God. This is the way of evangelization in modern day Japan.

We also hear reports from the field that local people and local government

41

officials call our volunteers "Mr." or "Ms. Caritas." The Church was in the area with the local people before the disaster. The Church was in the area with the local people during the disaster. And the Church will remain in the area with the local people after the disaster. This is all because the Church is part and parcel of local community. The Church, including outsiders such as "Mr. or Ms. Caritas" will remain in the disaster-hit area as member of the community, being animators among the local residents, creating hope and courage for the future, and in doing so being a witness to the gospel message.

Panel Discussion
Holistic Gospel Ministry

Masanori Kurasawa

Introduction

It is my privilege to be a panelist for the Great East Japan Earthquake International Theological Symposium. We gather together in order to deeply understand its meaning, widely extend our cooperative work through many Christian denominations and organizations, expand our centennial vision for the evangelization of post-disaster Japan, and share this vision with the next generation. I will speak on three related themes.

How We Understand and Speak of the March 11 Disaster Theologically

We were reminded of the Bible verse "though the earth give way and the mountains fall into the heart of the sea, though its waters roar and foam and the mountains quake with their surging" (Psalm 46:2–3, NIV) when it became reality during the largest earthquake (magnitude 9.0) and the highest tsunami in Japanese history. 18,524 people died or are missing as a result (January 14, 2014 data). This reality challenges us with the question "How God the Creator can be trusted as our refuge and strength, an ever-present help at the moment of distress and heartbreak?" In staying close to this reality, the cooperative effort and love of Christians working together with the suffering will show Japan our God and speak of His grace.

This incident rocked not only the earth and sea but also our very being and way of thinking. Human beings had become boastful and overconfident in the progress of human technology. Thus the word "*soteigai*" describing the disaster as "beyond the scope of our assumptions" and "unexpected" sprang to the lips of many. The disaster challenged our idea that we are able to control all areas of life, and it taught us that we are finite. It also reminds us to stand in awe and wonder at how nature can in an instant swallow up and take away our life. Even our huge man-made embankments could not hold back the tsunami, and our best infrastructure could not thwart the horrible accident at the Fukushima First Nuclear Power Plant. We need to reconsider in the present context the meaning of God's command to "subdue and rule over all the creatures of the universe" (Genesis 1:26, 28) and set a framework for fulfilling this God-entrusted task.

The church can respond to the challenge given, shaking off the way we thought and acted in the past. It can demonstrate Christian "welfare" in this time as it supports the sufferers and so contributes to the local community. Responding to this challenge, Tokyo Christian University (TCU) has begun a project, "The Theory and Practice of Christian Ministry in the Face of Natural Disasters," sponsored by the John Templeton Foundation. The three-year project seeks to develop comprehensive care studies from four perspectives, the physical, mental, social, and spiritual. The project will establish research groups corresponding to three questions: one on natural theology, another on the ethics of caring, and the third on Christianity and local community. Seminars, workshops, and a symposium will be planned, and reports of these meetings will be published.

How the Evangelicals Have Been and Will Continue be Involved with the Wounded Society through the Earthquake-Tsunami Disaster

The Lausanne Covenant (1974) affirms that Christian mission includes both evangelism and social responsibility. It offers Evangelicals a new avenue for holistic mission, rather than simply the old evangelism-based mission. The evangelical church has in part transitioned into actively engaging in social action and pursuing equity and justice, and is engaged in serving society through education and social work. Many Christians believe that the Gospel needs to be communicated through words and deeds that transform society. While it is undeniable that the church in general remains inward looking, the March 11 disaster pushed the church out into the community. The churches suffered together with the afflicted people. They became a hub for relief goods, transfer points for human networks and open spaces for suffering people. The churches have begun to better deal with the reality of life and death and the meaning of suffering alongside communities and individuals suffering and facing an uncertain future.

To meet urgent needs for relief and reconstruction, especially churches in the disaster-affected areas have cooperated not only with Christian churches and organizations, but also with local caregivers and community officials. They have become a part of regional alliances, and become more solidly rooted in the community. It is my hope that "a theology of cooperation" will surface as churches in the local affected areas consider the basic questions of which organizations and people to cooperate with, what kind of work to do and to what extent to work together, what values and purposes to be motivated by, and how long to be involved in relief efforts. These experiences and theology would be helpful in the event of a future anticipated large-scale earthquake. There needs to be cooperation between churches and communities in helping the afflicted, especially elderly, children, and foreigners. Furthermore, the Church can contribute to mental care for people in need in the community. The disaster has led us to consider a practical theology of the "holistic ministry of the Gospel," one learned in context, rather than transplanting familiar, preexisting theories into the field. There is a real need for each member of the Church to deeply understand the Gospel and live it out so that Jesus Christ the Savior could be revealed through them.

How We Proclaim the Gospel

Providing mental care, especially to help children and seniors recover from the disaster, has become a primary concern. The Humanitarian Disaster Institute of Wheaton College has set up a training program with a psychological approach to help those who support disaster victims. The people providing such support through Christian social work and relief organizations tend to specialize in their own area or profession. They need wisdom and innovative ideas for proclaiming the spiritual dimensions of the Gospel in and through their holistic ministry. It can be said that the Gospel can easily be proclaimed through the Church's "work of love." But even this requires scrupulous attention. Unless it gains the trust of the people it is supporting, the Church often faces a backlash of misunderstanding

One of our TCU graduates, Rev. Yoichi Fujiyabu, serves at Shirahama Baptist Christ Church in Wakayama. He continues the former pastor's "telephone lifeline (Inochi no Denwa)" counseling work, and his work includes suicide prevention and helping people gain independent living skills. Rev. Fujiyabu lives in a share house, where he leads daily devotions. He desires that the share house residents understand the meaning of life, and also learn how to live independently. Fujiyabu negotiates and networks with local officials to help his housemates find employment. In addition, the church in which Rev. Fujiyabu is serving has established a small restaurant operated by those who live in the share house, and from their earnings they offer free lunch boxes to the poor. Some have become Christians through these ministries and are now serving and caring for newcomers to the house. NHK featured the efforts of Fujiyabu and Shirahama Baptist Christ Church in their series on *Professionals* and their work. Few churches, however, offer such holistic care for people in need.

The Mission Research Institute of the Japan Alliance Christ Church (fol. Domei) to which I belong has discussed the concept of and direction for a Christian mission to the Tohoku region (fol. The Tohoku mission). The purpose of the Tohoku mission is to offer holistic care for the people living along the Sanriku Coastline. There are three issues involved here. First, all Domei churches need to work together to provide financial, physical and spiritual support for the mission personnel and for each congregation. The mission will be there for the long run, meeting the needs of the local community with the Gospel and gaining the trust of the local people. Second, the Tohoku mission will be a new style of church plant, different from the traditional model of a pastor working within a church. This is because not so many people now live in the Sanriku Coastline region, and plans for reconstruction there are not clearly scheduled, nor are efforts well coordinated. Third, cooperative and shared ministries and humanitarian aid work by neighboring churches, denominations and Christian NGOs are greatly needed. Even though cooperative ministries have been at work since the disaster, more need be done in the afflicted areas to improve mutual understanding and build relationships of trust, the foundations of responsible assistance. The Domei wants to serve as a good neighbor, meeting physical, mental, social and spiritual needs, helping people know the

Gospel, and establishing a Christian fellowship.

Final Notes

Since the disaster, many volunteers have come from within and from outside the afflicted areas to help with relief, recovery and reconstruction efforts. Through such experiences, younger Christians, especially, have been encouraged by the people they were serving. The volunteer work made the young Christians think deeply about their way of life and thinking. The reality of the afflicted people pushed the young volunteers to take a long look at themselves and their casual way of life. Being with the afflicted has encouraged them to live their life with strength and determination. We hope that in the face of this painful disaster the bond between the younger generation among the afflicted and volunteers will continue to be reinforced and developed for the future. As the afflicted and the volunteers take each other's hands and work together for a better tomorrow, this mutual encouragement will contribute to long-term recovery and reconstruction of the afflicted areas.

The issue on the theme "Raising Leaders through Sufferings beyond Walls" has challenged the Christian churches to show the power of the Gospel to the people in Japan, especially in the afflicted areas. It is for sure a time of challenge, yet God Almighty, who raised Christ from the dead, gives meaning to our hardship, destroys the various dividing walls and brings courage and hope to the next generation.

Panel Discussion

The Japan Baptist Convention and the Great East Japan Earthquake and Tsunami Disaster

Michio Hamano

I am Michio Hamano, Assistant Professor at the Seinan Gakuin Department of Theology. I have been a member of the Japan Baptist Convention Great East Japan Earthquake and Tsunami Disaster Relief Committee (below as the Committee for East Japan) since the disaster struck.

I would like to introduce today, as time permits, the activities of the various churches of the Japan Baptist Convention, the Committee for East Japan and local relief committees, as well as my own reflections on the theological and missions aspects of the disaster.

Principles Guiding our Actions

The first month after the disaster struck was literally a life and death struggle, with everyone doing everything she or he could possibly do. Once the initial phase had passed, we felt the need for guiding principles that could place our actions within the work of the church and its mission. This would be especially important in the longer-term in explaining the relief efforts to people throughout Japan in areas not affected by the disaster, and in making appeals for help to overseas groups. In clarifying and sustaining our motivation, clarifying our guiding principles would be important for ourselves as well, as people charged with serving churches and as Christians who must explain why we are engaged in relief activities. From our experience in the Great Hanshin-Awaji Earthquake Disaster, we knew that acting from a position of good intentions, albeit very worthy, could soon be self-extinguishing. We knew we needed some guiding principles to sustain us through the long process of disaster relief and recovery.

48

The Committee for East Japan then decided on the following set of guiding principles. First, we chose as our guiding scripture II Corinthians 5:18–19, NIV:

All this is from God, who reconciled us to himself through Christ and gave us the ministry of reconciliation: that God was reconciling the world to himself in Christ, not counting people's sins against them. And he has committed to us the message of reconciliation.

We also put our guiding principles to words in two statements:

"Support the work of reconciliation." We will work for reconciliation between people and God, people and people, and people and all Creation in the creation of a new fellowship in the Gospel.

We will keep our eyes on the work of Jesus of the cross as it works amidst the pain, suffering and distress of the disaster-stricken areas as we share the life and hope of the resurrection while valuing the attitude of respect and learning in relationships with the people of the stricken areas.

These principles come from the belief that reconciliation is necessary if true reconstruction is going to be achieved. One can also look at this as the idea of reconciliation at the core of the theology of the cross. The subtitle of the symposium, "through Sufferings," only reaffirms the necessity of a theology of the cross. And, "beyond Walls" proclaims the necessity of reconciliation. The expression "Support the work of reconciliation" was in use before the disaster and was part of the Japan Baptist Convention Mid- to Long-Range Framework (2011-2020) statement: " 'Support the work of reconciliation': Formation and Mission of Baptist Churches Living Out the Gospel of Reconciliation." At the time, it was thought that the term "reconciliation" was particularly relevant in light of globalization, and since the disaster it has been especially helpful in disaster relief efforts.

Just how related are reconciliation and disaster relief efforts can, I think, be understood in some comments made soon after the disaster struck. The following passage was published in the magazine *Ministry* (*Christian News* (Kirisuto shimbunsha)):

What is reconciliation between God and Man? How can we argue for God in an era of "There is no God nor Buddha"? We should be cautious of a theology of glory that exalts in an "Almighty God." What is needed is a theology of the cross in which God suffers with us. There are many people in the stricken areas and elsewhere asking themselves, "Why did just I survive?" and are faced with survivor guilt. What is sought is the message of forgiveness and coming together found in the cross, as in the scripture, "Your life is holy in the eyes of God." At the same time, people will seek the message that "All has not ended" as seen in millennial hopes. It is important to be careful to say the Kingdom of God is something that comes when it does and not something that people can easily "create" themselves. Since the disaster, the opinion has been heard that "we must not stop human progress" and therefore we need simply to build sturdier nuclear reactors. However, the future does not hold definite answers. In these situations where proper burials are impossible, religious workers are met with demands for an appropriate message. That message is found in millennial hopes.

There is a need for a message of reconciliation between people as well. There is a need for a message that can bring together the victims of the disaster and disaster relief workers (although it is often impossible to clearly separate these two identities). That message will arise from the specific, concrete actions of disaster relief, and the disaster relief efforts themselves will in turn gain power from that same message. Within the process of reconciliation there is also "judgment." In the human suffering of the nuclear disaster, there is a need for language that raises the question of the relationship between victimizers and victims. There is no avoiding responsibility for the direct victimizers, the "Nuclear Power Village" (the electrical power companies and the government authorities). At the same time, there is a need for language that questions each and every one of us and which seeks to transform the existing relationship in which "smoothing out the wrinkles around the nuclear power plant enables big city urban life." These issues can also be seen in the problems surrounding Okinawa and globalization. Furthermore, ignorance of radiation has brought about a discrimination against the Fukushima area such that we need a new language based on newer, accurate knowledge. And we need new language that questions the export of nuclear reactors by Japan to other Asian countries and that questions the nuclear industry-sided government's interests in money and profit and maintaining military power.

And, we need a message of reconciliation between God and Creation. Is it possible to say that "disaster is another act of God's creation?" Tsunami, earthquakes, nature and its phenomena, these are not God. Creation is itself not complete and is awaiting its own reconciliation with God. There is reconciliation between people and the whole of creation as well. There is a need for a message to address the slaughter of farm animals in the nuclear evacuation areas, the globally affecting scale of nuclear contamination of the ocean and the nuclear contamination of the atmosphere.[1]

The Great East Japan Earthquake and the Tsunami Disaster Relief Committee and its Activities

I will now address the kind of organization we formed and what kind of activities we have pursued in light of these guiding principles. The Committee for East Japan in 2013 is comprised of seven sections. The first section is concerned with the development of overall plans and with their theological aspects. The second section is involved in supporting churches in the stricken areas. This section liaisons with locally-based church-organized organizations outside the Committee for East Japan. The third section is the Tono Volunteer Center. This center coordinates the work of volunteers from around Japan as well as student volunteers from Seinan Gakuin University and Tokyo Women's University. This center, however, will be closing in 2014, and volunteer-related efforts will be undergoing some change. The fourth sections centers on aiding churches in the stricken areas. This is aid for those church members, church facilities, and pastors most directly impacted by the disaster. The fifth section, which I am currently heading, deals with issues arising from the nuclear disaster. This section is now providing child-care programs, health checkups by physicians, and so-called "nuclear decontamination" efforts. The sixth section provides valuable disaster-relief information both within Japan and internationally. Finally, the seventh section manages buildings and tools related to relief efforts.

The local relief committee I just mentioned comprises three teams, the Aomori-Iwate Team, the Miyagi Team and the Fukushima Team. These team members come from the membership of local churches, but their aim is to help rebuild local communities through attentive and caring relationships with local citizens and through aid to those in temporary housing. In this way, we have been working "beyond Walls" and toward further reconciliation.

This work beyond walls can be seen in fundraising efforts as well. As of August 2013, the Committee for East Japan has collected ¥212,229,365 in donations, 48% of which have been from overseas. We are also grateful to the many people who have come to the stricken areas to help from churches around the world. We can truly see an ongoing fulfillment of the work of God's reconciliation.

Issues

Not only has the Committee for East Japan received donations from churches abroad, but we have also received valuable advice as well. For example, at the 2012 Malaysia meeting of Asian-Pacific Baptist Fellowship relief-related personnel and Christian workers, we were able to gain much from the valuable lessons of long years of experience of people from various countries in relief efforts over a wide region. For example, there are language barriers that present problems in Japan different from those faced in other countries. It was also pointed out that sometimes it is difficult for those offering aid to have that aid accepted by others. It may be difficult to offer aid, aid workers may be isolated and alone, it may be difficult to achieve sustainable aid, and it may be difficult to form alliances across generational boundaries, all of which are particular issues facing churches in their relief efforts.

There are still other issues. The Committee for East Japan held both in 2012 and 2013 the "Forum to Address Missions and Theological Implications Arising from the East Japan Earthquake, Tsunami and Nuclear Reactor Disaster." We used those opportunities to take a moment to ask ourselves about the Biblical and missions implications of our relief efforts. Five main points can be made from these discussions. [2]

The first main point that can be made is the defeatism of the "either evangelism or aid" two-dimensional dichotomy. Any approach must be holistic and involve both aspects.

The second point was the importance of understanding and realizing the gospel of reconciliation.

The third point surrounded the question of the priesthood and prophecy of the church. The church must act both as a priest in the world and, on the other hand, must act as a prophet for a counter-culture. In any situation, which aspect to emphasize is an important question.

The fourth point considered the role of the theology of the cross with the caution that such an attitude not lean to "beautifying sacrifice" but rather to a reconsideration of how might the judgment of sin and the following forgiveness be considered.

Finally, the fifth point concerned cooperative missions and the position that emphasizes church autonomy within the historical Baptist framework. For example, evacuating the Fukushima churches might fall under a mission of the church. In such a case, the position of church autonomy should not become one of church isolation, but such autonomy should be maintained within a context of mutual cooperation. What is needed is the creation of relations whereby self-sufficiency supports cooperation and cooperation supports self-sufficiency.

As we were considering these issues at the 2013 forum, and as we had the feeling that the greatest burden of needs from the stricken areas was yet to come, we began asking what would be the best form of sustainable aid to churches and what the missions and theological foundations would be. My own view in light of the five points above is that, in order to provide sustainable aid, we must move from a theology of the cross to a theology of reconciliation, from priesthood to prophesy, from consolation to recognition of sin, not doing away with what has come before but expanding upon it. That is, we must move "through Sufferings" "beyond Walls." And in overcoming the barriers, we must rely not on the bathing warmth of the "Light of the World" but on the severity that is the "Salt of the Earth." That is because, in reference to the report of the Second Forum to Address Missions and Theological Implications Arising from the East Japan Earthquake, Tsunami and Nuclear Reactor Disaster, "what must not be overlooked is that the disaster is not just a singular disaster but the combination of many problems. In particular, the "nuclear problem" is actually the sum of many various problems facing Japanese society at this time. [. . .] We must recognize that it is not simply an environmental problem, but involves problems of politics, economics, international order and rising militarism all in one."[3]

This requires a rethinking of our values and ways of seeing the world. To borrow the words of the World Council of Churches: "Reconciliation is an objective to be achieved as well as a process,"[4] and inherent in that process is "repentance and justice."[5]

At the same time, churches must reconsider themselves. That is, the plight of nuclear workers, for example is related to the pursuit of greater power and higher efficiency, but the same outlook is also used in efforts to bring the next generation into the church such that the church has adopted a similarly opportunistic "liabilities and opportunities" approach which must be seriously re-examined.

Beyond Walls, toward the Next Generation

There will be an overcoming of the barriers as we follow a path of reconciliation that includes self-reflection. One outcome of the disaster relief efforts, among them being the "Forum to Address Missions and Theological Implications Arising from the East Japan Earthquake, Tsunami and Nuclear Reactor Disaster," has been the growth of an ecumenical fellowship. Such a growing ecumenicalism will further the work of reconsidering our values and world views resulting in relations that go beyond the more narrow meanings of disaster aid. For example, to help the victims of the nuclear disaster it is necessary to appeal to the government and various organizations to make public various related disaster-related information, and this has led to opposition to the Act on Protection of Specified Secrets. There are actually a great number of trusting pastors who would not have come into contact with each other without the pressing need for relief efforts, and one result of this coming together, for which we are grateful, has been the "Pastors Conference against the Act on Protection of Specified Secrets."

As we overcome the barriers, we will be moving into that new generation. Seinan Gakuin University where I work in in Fukuoka is far from the stricken areas, yet in 2013 nine teams totaling at least 100 students including the theological department students have participated in volunteer relief efforts. They have been enlarging alliances with students of Tohoku Gakuin University as well as other universities. In their summary meeting they all said, "We have gathered valuable hints as to how to lead our lives forthwith." Those who have experienced a reconsideration of their values and worldview will create a new world and will be bound together in their anticipation of the coming Kingdom of God.

One challenge I feel we will be facing is how to share what has happened in the nuclear disaster with younger generations. The Committee for East Japan has adopted a policy of not sending volunteers under age 40 into the radiation control areas where radiation is still being leaked. That means we will not be sending youth volunteers to Fukushima and Koriyama. If there is going to be a change in values and worldview, it is important for people to learn together about what is happening in Fukushima, but not being able to travel there is the difficulty. However, even if we cannot see the problem for ourselves or reach out and touch the problem, through our words of faith we can feel the pain of others and can find there a hope that overcomes the suffering. The opportunities and challenges are great, and this is a road that I look forward to walking with you.

1) Michio Hamano, "Thy Will be done on Earth as it is in Heaven," *Ministry* Vol. 10 (Kirisuto shinbunsha, 2011), 63–64.

2) Kanou Yoshitaka, "Reflections on the Forum." Japan Baptist Convention Research & Training Institute for Missions ed. *Forum I to Address Missions and Theological Questions Raised by the Great East Japan Earthquake and Tsunami Disaster: What has the Church Heard and Said?* (Japan Baptist Convention Great East Japan Earthquake and Tsunami Disaster Committee, 2012), 68–73.

3) Sawook Park, "Reflecting on the 'Great Disaster Forum II.'" Japan Baptist Convention Great East Japan Earthquake and Tsunami Disaster Committee's *Forum II to Address Missions and Theological Questions Raised by the Great East Japan Earthquake and Tsunami Disaster: The Church Listens "to the Bible, the Situation and Experience"* (2014), 138.

4) World Council of Churches World Missions and Evangelism Committee, ed., Kenji Kanda, ed., Makoto Kato, transl., *Reconciliation and Healing: Evangelism and Missions in the 21st Century* (Kirisuto shinbunsha, 2010), 42.

5) Ibid, 43.

Workshop Report
Workshop 1: Considerations in Psy...

Creating New Narrat...

Akira Fujikake

Two Principles

1. The psychological renewal of ...

When I read Genesis 45 fre... I see a clear picture of the elderly Jacob experienci... the midst of great suffering and trials. Jacob hear... n, Joseph, whom he had long thought dead, is alive ... not bring himself to believe this, and remains langu... to grasp the reality of his situation and recover fro... things: first, a new narrative; second, a ritual.

Jacob hears the whole st... Joseph (the story of God's providence) from the p... ...ded that his son was surely dead. Hearing a comple... one he had imagined, Jacob faces the task of rewriti... head up to this point.

Then Jacob is shown the ... . The lavish grandeur of the chariot, dispelling all ... at Joseph truly sat in authority in Egypt. First, thi... ...cob feel the reality of Joseph's charge to "take this ... in Egypt as quickly as you can," and second, it spu... he journey. With these two pieces in order, an encouraged and empowered Jacob sets outs for Egypt.

2. Two necessary principles

We, too, at turning points in life, change our pace and try to encourage ourselves, but things do not always go so easily. For example, should we only look back on our past, although we may discover some things, the task of looking back seems never-ending. Looking back fails to result in setting out anew or making a conclusive decision, and our daily lives do not change. We lack here a ritual. On the other hand, we may give ourselves a reward, or establish a special anniversary day. Such events alone, however, end in a short-lived celebration. We lack here a new narrative.

A new narrative and ritual: with these two in place, we find ourselves empowered and able to actually set out towards a new way of life. In dealing with the earthquake disaster as well, I believe this will become an important point.

Psychological Considerations

1. A new narrative

When we relate with victims of disaster, it is important that we help facilitate their making of a "new narrative." Experiencing a life crisis makes a person reflect on his or her life and give meaning to the crisis. Examining our experience with all seriousness and seeking to interpret it, we can see something like the dots of our life connect one by one. We are made aware, as it were, of our own life narrative.

Narrative here does not mean a fictional story. It means you making sense of your own life and the world that surrounds you, and understanding this in your own words. There is no model answer. Each person must examine self and situation, seeking the words to compose their own story.

To make one's own narrative, it is no good merely to lose oneself in deep thought. One must speak with God, and speak to others. As a person speaks and listens, they become aware of their own thoughts, gaining new insight and new power to move. In this process, the one helping needs to keep some things in mind.

1) Do not hurry the making of a narrative. 2) Do not be bound in narrative making by ready-made model answers. 3) Once a narrative has been formed, do not try to lock it in place, but accept its constant revision. 4) When multiple, conflicting narratives exist, do not be in a hurry to discard one, but rather, respecting all the narratives, wait for them to become integrated. 5) Expect a narrative with the disaster at its center to become one's life narrative. 6) Accept not only the narratives of individuals, but also and equally those of the family, community, and nation.

2. Rituals

When relating to disaster victims, it is important to consider how they might gain access to "rituals." For both mind and body, there need be limits and milestones. For a new start, rituals with religious meaning in the wider sense are necessary. A ritual is not just a formality, but connects to deep experiences of the soul. Here are some points for those who help to keep in mind.

1) Cherish the rituals that protect our daily life. 2) Cherish the kinds of rituals that provide recreational diversions. 3) Do not only use existing rituals, but also create new ones. Also, as helpers deepen their involvement with disaster victims, helpers must also create within themselves new narratives and rituals.

Making rituals is not only a task for the individual. The individual and family, the local community, and the nation must at intervals make rituals. The Christian community must also share ideas together and look to make a new start. The church and the believers must see the need to pray and seek greater wisdom.

(translated by Brian Byrd)

Workshop Report
Workshop 1: Considerations in Psychological Counseling
Care for Stress of the Heart and Soul

Hajime Hori

Memento Mori

As mass media covered the Great East Japan Earthquake Disaster fever-ishly from every angle and pundits added their earnest commentary, the Medieval Latin watchword, "*memento mori*" came to my mind: "remember (that you have) to die." *Memento mori* calls us to live each day to the fullest, realizing that we do not know when death may come. We must take this truth, this obvious truth, to heart.

Normally, however, *memento mori* does not enter our thoughts. Its reality hits only when war or natural disasters strike, causing massive injuries and loss of life, or traffic accidents or sudden death catch us totally unprepared. So it was with the earthquake disaster, which raised my *memento mori* to a level many times the norm. The earth kept shaking and rolling, and though it was actually soon over, I thought that this might be our last day.

Following the disaster, I also felt more strongly the words of Thomas à Kempis so often quoted in sermons and talks. He prayed

> Who can know what a single day might bring. Therefore, O God, help me to
> live each day as though it were my last in this world. I know that we cannot say
> that any day might not be the last.*

The importance of "living each day as though it were our last" gets lost in the midst of our busy activities. The instant and painful death of so many, however, has forced me to think again and think realistically. Sermons also have reflected this awareness of and awakening to the deep realities of life and death.

Anyone Can Suffer from Stress Disorder

Memento mori turns my thoughts almost automatically to my own work as a pastoral counselor. As people see and experience a disaster of this scale, and as the media drives home its shock and horror again and again, peoples' hearts are wounded. This in itself can be called a disaster. The technical term "stress disorder" loomed large in my heart. Although I cannot speak in much detail here, I hope that what I say might be of some help to those here.

Stress disorder affects those that go through an intense or life-threatening experience, such as this earthquake disaster. Seeing and reliving the traumatic scenes deeply wounds the heart and leads to strong emotions such as fear or powerlessness. The "stress reactions" can be described as follows:

1) Memories of the earthquake that replay over and over again in the mind, causing a person to feel sick and down. This happens when seeing news broadcasts, or visiting again the place where one experienced the earthquake.

2) Not wanting to think or talk about the earthquake—about earthquake related news, for example; avoiding the earthquake as a topic of conversation.

3) Nervous tension, reacting with heightened sensitivity to things such as small noises.

4) Feeling guilty, anxious, depressed.

5) Displaying various kinds of physical symptoms such as shortness of breath, palpitation, difficulty with digestion, hands and legs shaking or trembling, and sleep disorders.

These emotional and physical symptoms occur not only with natural disasters, but also with traffic accidents or being the victim of a crime, for example. Although people do react differently, anyone can be affected. To give one example, one victim that I met surprised me by talking so cheerfully about things that had no relation to the earthquake. This clearly can be seen as one type of stress reaction.

In some cases a victim may react so strongly that their pain and suffering comes out even in dreams. They may want to avoid activities, places, and even people that remind them of their wounds. These symptoms may go on for more than a month. Many people are experiencing what are known as Post-Traumatic Stress Disorder (PTSD).

Self-care First

When the level of stress is high, the resultant PTSD, depression, or anxiety may require professional help. However, I would also like to suggest "self-care," things that you can do for yourself.

1) First, do not push yourself too hard. Do not think that you have to push yourself even though you have little energy, or that you have to be useful for others.

2) Do not try to bottle up feelings of fear or anxiety, sadness or anger. Christians can speak to God who hears our cries. Look to the Psalms for the best examples here.

3) Enjoy yourself! When we experience stress, our emotions in a way shut down, and the color drains out of our daily lives, leaving them black and white. To little by little return to normal, do the things that you like— music, arts, walking, etc.

4) If it is not too painful, try reading books that make you think. The good thing about reading is the way it can change our outlook and way of thinking, and thus calm us emotionally. Reading does influence our emotions.

5) People are the greatest source of comfort. We cannot always count on family and friends; however, we should be with people that do not wound us, those with whom we feel at ease. Even Paul asks his friend to "refresh my heart in Christ." (Philemon 20, NIV) When a person knows that there is someone that will never forget them, they will experience true support for their heart. I want people to know that more than anything else, God with us is the greatest support our hearts and souls can know.

(＊) from Veronica Zundel, ed. *Eerdmans Book of Famous Prayers*, 1984.

(translated by Brian Byrd)

Workshop Report
Workshop 2: Support and Ministry

The Dilemma of Mission in Tohoku:
Balancing Physical Relief and Spiritual Salvation

Makoto Suzuki

Introduction

The many Christian relief groups working to bear witness in the disaster area face this dilemma: how to offer disaster victims both physical relief and the good news of spiritual salvation.

The Dilemma of the Disaster Victims

Disaster victims receiving support from religious organizations tend to harbor a deep-set wariness towards religion. At the same time, having lost family, friends, and livelihood instantly through the disaster, they face questions of "the meaning of life" and "guilt for having survived." They feel deep spiritual hunger, and expect something from religion. They know that simply receiving material assistance is not enough. Thus, they are caught in the dilemma of needing the support that religion offers, yet being extremely cautious in opening themselves to an unfamiliar religion.

In the first stage of their relief activities, many of the Christian groups made an effort not to offer material support as though in exchange for interest in Christianity. Such relief work has made a favorable impression on those in the affected areas. The problem is what to do from now.

The Dilemma within the Church

The earthquake disaster hit at a time when a sense of stagnation hovered over the work of mission in Japan. Churches tend to average around thirty members. From before the earthquake, fewer students had been entering seminary, and church school programs had been in decline, paralleling an ongoing decrease in the Christian population.

Disaster support by the church raises this question: Can the church take up the challenge of practicing the Bible's teaching of love for neighbor, providing support in this disaster, while at the same time confronting its own vulnerability? Three years have passed since the earthquake, and a struggle has begun between the pastors of churches involved in relief activities and their church members. Can long-term relief activities continue to exist alongside the need to build up the supporting church? Churches supporting relief organizations are also in the process of seeking to discern what their outlook should be from now.

Beyond this, the nuclear contamination experienced by and still threatening many cities, towns, and villages in Fukushima makes this disaster completely different from a natural one, and adds its oppressive weightiness to the tsunami and earthquake damage. Nuclear contamination will shackle rebuilding efforts for a long time to come. The Fukushima churches and the churches giving support there confront a dilemma different from that in the Miyagi and Iwate Prefecture disaster areas.

In Fukushima churches located near the evacuated areas and exposed to nuclear contamination, church members who fled the area and those who for various reasons were forced to remain have differing perceptions of the situation. Pastors with small children, for example, who temporarily left their homes to protect their families experienced criticism from church members who were left behind. Pastors in Fukushima thus continue to deal with theological issues concerning the nature of their calling that cannot be discussed in terms of a simple spirit of martyrdom. Can pastors who live away from the affected areas really consider these issues as someone else's problems?

The Gap between Traditional Theological Frameworks and the Reality of Mission in Japan

Working primarily in the towns of Minamisanriku and Ishinomaki, we came to know the existence of a traditional community structure in the Tohoku coastal areas called the "*ko*." Due to population decline and aging, even before the earthquake the communities (*ko*) providing bonding and support for the people in these regions were breaking down. The earthquake will only spur the collapse of these areas' communities. We can conjecture that the nature of traditional folk society will change. This change will hit the aging and the weak especially hard. The collapse of folk society's structures, which functioned in ways that went beyond the government, will lead to the loss of means to protect the weak in society.

Will churches involved in relief work or beginning mission work because of the disaster be able to build Christian community in place of the traditional communities? This is one of the questions we will face.

A Disaster Victim's Question: "Would you Christians become Buddhists in fifteen minutes?"

What is being questioned here is our understanding of the gospel as Protestants, and especially as Evangelicals. Are we not being called to reexamine this understanding? The so-called evangelical churches have distanced themselves from the social gospel group, placing the greatest emphasis on preaching the gospel, on "evangelism" and "the salvation of souls." Their mission has based its evangelical efforts on "subjective faith" and "personal development," sensing "preaching the message of salvation" to be its calling and its highest value.

On one occasion, disaster victims were gathered for a meeting in the disaster area. The evangelist who had come from abroad for relief work finished his message, "My listeners, if your life was to end today, do you have the conviction that you would go to heaven? Believe now in Jesus Christ and make 'salvation' your own. Get in your hand a ticket to heaven" he called, seeking decisions for faith.

One person heard this evangelical message with shoulders sagging and head down. After the meeting, he asked a missionary that had been helping with relief work. "Sir, you're a Christian, aren't you. If this is the case, I want to ask you whether if you heard a Buddhist priest speak like this, could you, in fifteen minutes, become a Buddhist?"

Telling this story at a later meeting, I suggested that, "for mission in Japan, rather than condemning other religions, it is important for evangelicals to have a willingness to dialogue with them." One pastor in the evangelical group argued back, "If the Holy Spirit works, can a person not be saved instantaneously? These

65

'non-Christians' are in the hand of Satan." I suspect that this kind of under-standing is rather common among evangelicals.

From Mission to Witness

Our Christian network that provides supports in Minamisanriku emphasizes "witnessing for Christ by coming alongside to engage in dialogue." We seek to witness in our region and with a gospel that understands our area and Tohoku. We are living out the love of Christ as his disciples not through our words, but through our deeds. As we go about our relief work and mission, and through symposiums like this one, I would like us to continue to build up and strengthen our theological understanding.

* Due to space constraints, I was unable to write in detail. I used the following works as references.
* Kazo Kitamori, *Nihonjin no kokoro to Kirisutokyo* (Christianity and the Japanese Heart) (Yomiuri Shimbunsha, 1973).
* Keishin Inaba and Hiroyuki Kurosaki, ed., *Shukyo to social capital 4: Shinsai fukko to shukyo* (Christianity and Social Capital 4: Religion and the Rebuilding After the Earth-quake) (Akashi Shoten, 2013).
* Kosuke Koyama, *Suigyu shingaku* (Water Buffalo Theology). Translated by Koji Moriizumi. (Kyobunkan, 2011).
* Bruce W. Winter, *Seek the Welfare of the City* (Eerdmans, 1994).
* Information on the current situation of churches in Fukushima was based on interviews with pastors in the Fukushima Christian Association.

(translated by Brian Byrd)

Workshop Report
Workshop 2: Support and Ministry

Miyagi Mission Network

Yukikazu Otomo

Background

The Great East Japan Earthquake Disaster on March 11, 2011 left 20,000 people dead or missing. Within the first week or two, Christian emergency relief organizations and churches within Japan and from abroad were working feverishly to send supplies and personnel to the affected areas.

We had learned through the Bible from before the disaster that the mission of the church involved social ministry and evangelism, and that as Jesus Christ was preaching the gospel, he helped the poor and the weak and healed the sick and demon possessed. Also, the church in Jerusalem in the time of the apostles distributed food to the poor as it evangelized. The book of James teaches that good works accompany true faith. The spoken gospel is important, but when accompanied by good works, this touches the heart of the other person. In other words, the model for mission in the time of the apostles was social ministry and evangelism moving forward together as do two wheels on the axle of a car.

Before March 11, those living around our churches had the food, clothing, and shelter that they needed. We could not do mission as in the time of the apostles. After March 11, supplies for daily life were lacking, and many supplies and personnel were sent through the churches. In other words, one of the wheels on the axle was turning. I thought that we had to get the other wheel in motion.

I had been in a network from before the earthquake with a number of pastors who were doing church planting. After the earthquake, we prayed concerning evangelism in the disaster areas. We felt led to start by establishing the Miyagi Mission Network, and held our first meeting in September of 2011, six months after the earthquake. We had expected thirty people, but ended up with eighty attending, and realized that people were concerned not just for relief activities, but also for evangelism.

As we prepared to move forward in mission in the disaster areas, we thought to use the Great Hanshin-Awaji (Kobe) Earthquake as our reference point. However, no appropriate model existed, so we as members of the network put our heads together, and listening to the Lord, we have been led to where we are today.

We first divided the areas in Miyagi hit by the disaster into five blocks, each of which could be covered by car in an hour, and began our work. The networks begun in each of these blocks are now growing little by little. We hold a general network meeting every month where each block reports on planned events, relief activities, and other matters. Members also share about the various evangelical efforts underway in the disaster areas.

Purpose

To do mission work in disaster-hit Miyagi Prefecture by setting up a network of churches, Christians, missionary organizations, and missionaries that desire to do church planting inside and outside the disaster-affected areas in order to establish ecclesia (house churches, small churches). (See Matthew 16:18)

Network Guidelines

A network for mutual encouragement and support that does church planting by coaching:

1) Respect the independent activities of each church organization and denomination.
2) Share information about events like evangelistic meetings and concerts, and also concerning seekers.
3) Hold regular meetings that include church planting workers and their supporters.
4) Hold network-sponsored mission rallies several times a year.
5) Cooperate as a network in the raising up of church (ecclesia) leaders.

68

6) Divide Miyagi Prefecture into different blocks and appoint a leader and assistant for each block.

7) Receive information about relief activities of churches and individuals from outside the prefecture, and about those who become seekers through those activities.

8) When an ecclesia is birthed, leave its denominational affiliation up to the ecclesia.

9) Allow an ecclesia to remain in the network for as long as it so desires.

10) The goal of this network is to raise up a great number of churches, so that anyone living in Miyagi Prefecture can easily attend a church, and with this as a model, to expand into an East Japan Mission Network and an All-Japan Mission Network, so that through the increase in churches throughout Japan we can evangelize the nation.

Issues

1) Disaster Area Mission Research Institute

Major earthquakes are predicted to hit Japan in the future. We seek the creation of a Disaster Area Mission Research Institute to collect data useful for mission work in future times of crisis.

2) The creation of networks in other areas

In the first Mission Network Forum held February 10, 2014 in Sendai, about thirty pastors from the four prefectures most affected by the disaster attended. It was decided to continue such meetings, but funding is necessary.

3) Christian burial place

Most of those who came to faith through the disaster live and work in farming and fishing villages. For these people, the presence or absence of a place for burial is a serious concern. Having a burial place available in each area makes it easier to make a confession of faith, and to live a life of faith.

Conclusion

Doing mission in the disaster-affected areas in Japan has just begun, and it remains a largely unknown field. Regardless of what the result may be, we desire through the network to build relationships with disaster victims and give witness through evangelistic activities, and to learn together. Through this sharing, we will come to understand the method of evangelism and the types of churches most suitable for the disaster victims.

(translated by Brian Byrd)

Workshop Report

Workshop 3: Rituals

How to Engage with Rites for the Dead and Traditional Folkways

Takashi Yoshida

Introduction: Why This Topic?

When we discuss missions in Japan, and in particular, missions in rural Japan, we must consider how to engage with rites for the dead and traditional folkways. I would like to attempt here to address the topic not in terms of cultural contextualization, as is often done, but in terms of the realities that Tohoku churches have been facing since the Great East Japan Earthquake in 2011.

Working in the disaster area where the casualties, including the number of missing people, totaled nearly 20,000, we have learned the crucial importance of burying the victims respectfully, at times in collaboration with ministers of other faiths. What is the meaning of rites for the dead? What is the significance for Christians, and more specifically, for pastors as religious leaders to be involved in those rites? Through carefully contemplating these questions, I believe new light will be shed upon the topic.

The Earthquake Disaster and Rites for the Dead: Efforts by Tohoku HELP

The Sendai Christian Alliance Disaster Relief Network (Tohoku HELP), which I am serving as a representative, was founded a week after the March 11, 2011 disaster. During those early days, an unexpected question was posed: "Should we somehow pay respect to the deceased?" Later it became clear that this question was asked out of an awareness of the need of survivor care for family members of suicide victims. It was pointed out that if your loved one is suddenly taken away, grieving and giving them a proper burial will help greatly in coping with the loss.

Tohoku HELP and the local Buddhist Association jointly asked Sendai City for permission to minister to the dead. As a result, we were allowed to set up a religious consultancy office in a crematorium, to offer to perform simple funeral rites for free, and to provide free counseling in waiting rooms of the crematorium. The Miyagi Prefectural Association of Religious Organizations embraced the local government's response. They took the initiative of setting up the consultancy office and approved that the Sendai Buddhist Association and Tohoku HELP would jointly manage the office.

Thus started the Heart Counseling Room in the local crematorium. A Buddhist monk and a Christian minister (Protestant or Catholic) would be available at all times, to advise not only about funeral and burial rites, but also about medical and legal issues. The workers in the Heart Counseling Room agreed to be, first and foremost, ministers of presence for survivors, and never to coerce toward their religion. They would focus on the survivors' grief care as they participated in rites for the dead. They would keep in mind that this is a joint work with other religions and the local administrative office, and would always treat co-workers with respect. These were the primary guidelines agreed upon by all parties involved in the Heart Counseling Room.

Though the consultancy room in the crematorium was closed in May 2011, the collaborative work was valued so highly that it continued as a telephone counseling service. A radio program was then developed and has been aired until today under the title "Heart Counseling Room." Another spin-off is the launch of a course at Tohoku University, funded by donations, to develop clinical religious ministers (chaplains, in the Japanese context).

Biblical Examples of Rites for the Dead

What does the Bible say about the rites for the dead, and in particular, indigenous rites? Let us examine two representative examples in the Bible. First, we will look at the burial of Jacob, the father of the Israelites. Second, we take up the burial of Jesus.

1. Jacob's burial

Jacob ended his earthly life in Egypt. Genesis 50 describes his burial in detail. His body was embalmed by Egyptian physicians. Egyptians mourned, if only for the sake of formality, for 70 days (vv. 2–3), and sent off the body with great flourish for burial in the land of Canaan (v. 9) where a solemn funeral was conducted (v. 10) — so much so that the local Canaanites said, "This is a grievous mourning on the part of the Egyptians" (v. 11, NRSV).

This passage does not come across as a record of humiliation in that Jacob, an Israelite patriarch, was buried according to pagan customs. We should rather read it as a record of God's grace in which a former "nobody" grew in the Lord's mysterious guidance, to reach the end of his life in a grand manner, at least by earthly standards.

2. Jesus' burial

Jesus was also buried, quite naturally, in accordance with the Jewish burial customs of the day (John 19:38–42). He was not buried in a "Christian" manner. As a matter of fact, there were no rules regarding Christian funerals at that time, nor have there been up to today. Like the burial of Jacob, the burial of Jesus, made possible by the bold act of Joseph of Arimathea, is also recorded as a praiseworthy event (Mark 15:43).

The Whole Gospel

1. Human dignity

The two Scripture passages that we have looked at tell us that the Bible does not stipulate a set of rules for rituals surrounding death. The focus is not on indigenous customs but on the importance of burying the body in a respectful manner. Burying the body with respect allows people to remember the grace of God upon the deceased and to express their appreciation and love for the deceased. In other words, the body is not a mere decaying object, but the visible remains of someone who was created in the image of God (Genesis 1:27), and whose remains, therefore, should be treated with dignity.

2. Comfort to the grieving

When Jesus came across a funeral procession of the only son of a widow, he saw her and had compassion for her. He then dared to touch the casket, which was unclean according to Jewish law (Luke 7:11–14). When Lazarus died and

Jesus saw Martha at a loss and the villagers mourning, "he was greatly disturbed in spirit and deeply moved" (John 11:33). Jesus went so far as to weep (John 11:35). Here again, Jesus' primary attention goes to powerless people grieving the death of their loved one. As Jesus feels indignant about the death itself that caused people's sorrow, he stands close by the grieving people and shows God's power that overcomes death.

Jesus modeled how to "[r]ejoice with those who rejoice, weep with those who weep" (Romans 12:15). Jesus always shared the point of view with those who had fallen (Luke 10:36). He set his standards of conduct to living out the whole gospel, which seeks to heal human brokenness.

Conclusion: Roles of the Church and Christians on Earth (Particularly Ministers' Roles)

When discussing the roles of the Church and Christians on earth, the emphasis has often been placed on their prophetic role. Having experienced the earthquake disaster of 2011, God seems to have been teaching us that the priestly role is just as important. As religious ministers, we play the priestly role in remembering the dead, consoling surviving family members, and providing comfort to grieving people who are powerless in the face of death. Religions engage with people's souls at the deepest level. If we love people in their entirety, we need to respect their religious faith. Doing so does not necessarily mean categorically endorsing their religion or beliefs. When we are involved in rites for the dead or in traditional folkways, the most important point is where our heart is. I believe that holding such a viewpoint will open the way for religions to serve in the public arena. I also believe that through actively engaging with rites for the dead and traditional folkways, the uniqueness and power of the gospel of Jesus Christ will be clearly shown.

(translated by Brian Byrd)

Plenary Session
What Disasters Teach the Church

David Boan

Introduction

In March 2011, the Christian churches in Japan, along with the rest of the country, experienced an epiphany: Long held assumptions about safety, the community, and how to serve the Japanese people were, like many communities along Japan's north coast, overwhelmed by the tsunami.

Such disasters demand our attention and action. They are called natural disasters, but may also be called civic disasters as entire communities are disrupted or destroyed and along with them, people are killed or displaced and suffer terribly. These disasters call into question our relationship to the community and our responsibility as Christians. When so many government and private groups respond to this disaster, what is the proper role for the church? If the church acts as another relief agency, how does it maintain a distinct witness? What are the risks to the church of devoting scarce resources to the seemingly never ending cycle of disasters?

The response to disasters, both the immediate response and the long term recovery, has increasingly engaged the church and faith-based groups. The number of faith-based non-governmental organizations (NGOs) worldwide has grown significantly the past few decades. Supporting that growth has been the increasing willingness of governments and other funders to support faith-based groups, and in some countries, even directly fund churches for disaster care. This has been called the New Policy Agenda in which governments play less of a role in development while local actors, including churches and faith-based organizations, play a larger role (Hearn, 2002). For example, driven in part by the Charitable Choice provision of the George W. Bush administration, USAID

75

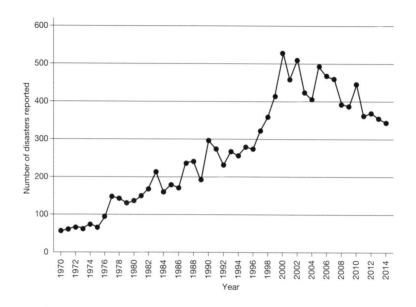

Graph 1: Frequency of Disasters Worldwide, 1970–2014

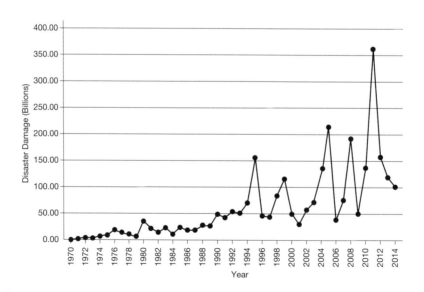

Graph 2: Disaster Damage (Billions) 1970–2014

What Disasters Teach the Church

funding to faith-based organizations between 2001 and 2005 rose to $1.7 billion (US. dollars.) Driving this trend is the recognition that there are people that government groups do not serve well or cannot reach. In contrast to government and large NGOs, churches are seen as typically well connected to their local community, and as such, valuable extenders of the work of governments and NGOs. Engaging churches started from seeing them as sources for recruiting volunteers, and then evolved into recruiting the churches themselves to do the work of the agency or NGO.

In tandem with these trends in faith-based organization engagement, there has been a dramatic rise in both the frequency of disasters (Graph 1) and the amount of disaster damage (Graph 2). While the reason for this increase is debated, whether it is because disasters are more intense or more people are in the path of disasters, the increase in destruction and lives lost is clear.

These multiple trends have been both an opportunity and a threat to the church. They provide valuable lessons for Japanese churches and seminaries asking such questions as what is a proper role for the church in disasters, is this something best left to government, and how do disasters relate to the basic mission of the church. The aim of this paper is to clarify these threats and their lessons so that other churches and congregations will be equipped to recognize them, and in that way address some of these questions. We then propose strategies with a clear theological basis that equip the church for disaster related ministry while minimizing risks to the church's essential mission.

The Mission of the Church

In order to understand the risks of engaging in disaster ministry we must first establish what exactly is it, that is being put at risk. We start with the proposition that there are defining tasks for the church, that is, tasks that go to the essence of the reason for the existence of the church. Anything that threatens these defining tasks needs to be approached with great care, if not avoided altogether. In the extreme, when these defining tasks are compromised, then the primary mission and identity of the church is compromised. We see three of these tasks as especially relevant to our discussion of disaster care: The proclamation of the church as the salt of the earth, the call to the church as the light of the earth (Matthew 5:13–16), and the repeated call throughout the Bible to serve the vulnerable (e.g. Matthew 25:35; Acts 10:4).

Salt penetrates the earth. The analogy to salt is to say that the church preserves the world and acts to protect it from corruption. Note that Jesus does not say He is the salt, he says His disciples are the salt, and not the salt of the church, the salt of the entire earth. He also does not say *become* salt, or *you should be salt*, but that you are salt (Bonhoeffer, p. 104). Therefore, our presence in the world is needed and expected. We are also cautioned that when a salt loses its taste, it then no longer has value (Matthew 5:13). This caution speaks to our main point, that anything that threatens the role of the church as the salt of the earth threatens the foundation of the church.

Light refers to visibility, being engaged in a way that is visible to others. Unlike salt, Christ does refer to Himself as light, and His followers are also to make their light visible to others. The work of the church is to be visible to the world.

But what kind of light? This question points us to exactly what is it that is to be visible. Bonhoeffer refers to these works as the work Christ has called all disciples to: serving the poor, peace, servitude, and the qualities of the beatitudes (Bonhoeffer, 1949).

In preserving the earth, and acting in a way that is visible to others, there is also a particular character to this work. Scripture is clear; we are commanded to do unto the least of these. We also have the parable of the Good Samaritan in acting when we see people suffering. This addresses the importance of serving the weak and vulnerable, with no reference to whether they are within the church. We are simply commanded to serve them wherever we may find them. Thus, it is natural for churches to be responsive in the event of disasters, and see this as an important area of ministry. The question we are examining is not whether to be responsive to a disaster, but rather how are we to respond in a way that is consistent with being salt, light, and compassionate to those in need?

This brings us to our central theme: In terms of disasters, we propose that the church must be engaged as the church, meaning in a way that serves the commandment to be salt, light and compassionate. There are ways to be involved that compete with and can do damage to the mission of the church. The church needs to understand the distinction.

We further propose that this speaks to the issue of what is known as "social gospel." There is a long-standing concern among conservative groups that engaging in serving the community creates the image of the church as a social agency and fails to correctly convey the message of the gospel. Our analysis supports this concern. Some argue that the liberal theology movement of the 1930s and 1940s did a poor job of developing the theological basis for social mission while reacting to conservative theology, thus creating an unnecessary schism between social ministry and evangelism (Metaxas, 2011). This speaks to the point we are making. Again, we are commanded to be salt and light, and to serve others in need, and so have no choice about engaging with the community, but how the church does it is the key issue.

Unfortunately, there are two sources of distortion in how we carry out this mission in regard to disasters: Our understanding and response to disasters and the church's relationship to other agencies, both government and private. We will now consider each of these distortions and the challenge they present so we can then formulate models of response that address these concerns.

Our Misperception of Disasters

When asked about disasters, the average person thinks of extreme events, e.g. tornadoes, tsunamis, earthquakes, etc. This is a bias to think of disasters as only those events that are unpredictable, extreme, and unusual. This bias is compounded by several related factors. First, the media focuses on extreme and exceptional events as most newsworthy. This is a brief focus, and soon the media is on to the next extreme event. Thus, we think disasters are also short lived. Further, the images from disasters are dramatic, clear and easily recalled. Consider the image of the ships swept inland by the tsunami, or the planes flying into the World Trade Center on 9/11. Events that are repeated in the media and associated with clear images seem to us to be more likely to happen. This is called the availability heuristic (Carroll, 1978). As a result of being presented with clear, dramatic images played over and again, people distort risks. In the US, people have a heightened awareness of terrorism and many people avoid flying, even though the risk of being killed by terrorism in the US is lower than the risk of dying from your pajamas being set on fire, lightening, bee stings, or peanut allergies (Pinker, 2011). Put another way, when we consider the likelihood of an event, or the degree of need, people are guided by the vividness of their imaginations and the frequency of hearing about something rather than by facts. Consider Graph 3 showing the reporting of disaster events by the New York Times (below). Clearly, there is intense interest in the first ten days, and then interest drops quickly.

The response to disasters, as measured by donations, follows a similar curve, with donations to the Haiti earthquake peaking less than three days after the event. In addition to suggesting the short attention for news, this short term focus reinforces the view that disasters are about the immediate crisis.

Graph 3: Number of News Reports on Haiti Earthquake

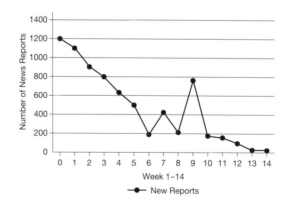

From our work in disaster ministries, we see several consequences of this crisis view: First, it defines the disaster by the immediate crisis and neglects long term consequences and needs. Focusing on the immediate crisis creates an approach to disaster driven by episodes of extreme events rather than long term

What Disasters Teach the Church

engagement. An episodic focus makes it very difficult to maintain a program as people lose interest and their skills decline. Further, it overlooks the very strength of the church and congregations, which is the long term presence in the community and connections to the most vulnerable as a result of serving those in need.

Second, like focusing on terrorism, these distortions cause us to overestimate risk from dramatic events and underestimate risk from less dramatic events. There are many disasters that have a major community impact, but are not associated with dramatic events. Influenza and other contagious diseases, like MRSA, are major threats that are not considered disasters, but kill many more people than extreme weather. Less dramatic weather events, or slowly unfolding events, like heat waves or the impact of climate change, gather less attention because they are not associated with clear, dramatic images that make it into the media.

Third, the focus on extreme events causes us to overlook who suffers from disasters in the long term because our attention comes to an end as the initial dramatic phase of disaster passes. Consider the following events:

In 2011 the largest outbreak of tornadoes occurred in the Southeast US. The worst of these struck Tuscaloosa Alabama where an EF5 tornado went through the suburbs. Of the more than 200 people killed, 60% were over age 55, and half of those over 80. 90% of the victims were active in their local church, and none of the churches had any plan for care of vulnerable people in a disaster.

In 2002, an ice storm in North Carolina knocked out power to 5 million people in the midst of winter. 34 people died, not from cold, but mainly from carbon monoxide poisoning. Most of those people were migrant workers from the south who had no experience with extreme cold and did not know the dangers of heating your home with barbeque or other open flame.

In 1997, Chicago experienced a major heat wave that killed 750 people over four days. Most of those people were elderly who lived in older, poorly insulated buildings in high crime areas. The deaths had as much to do with their social

81

situation and vulnerability as with the heat wave (Klinenberg, 2002).

Finally, consider the victims of the 2011 tsunami. Nearly two and one half years after the earthquake and tsunami 103,000 are reported still living in temporary housing with no prospects of rebuilding their homes.[1] The people in temporary shelters are predominantly over 60 and from the small coastal towns destroyed in the tsunami. These statistics and those above reveal that the vulnerable are not only vulnerable in terms of the immediate impact, but also the longer term impact of disasters. This is a pattern repeated with every disaster around the world: The vulnerable suffer most of the long term consequences.

These examples, and many others like them, point out several characteristics of our perception of disasters and risk:

Misperception #1 Disaster ministry means doing relief work.

This misperception results from seeing disaster work as relief work during the peak of the crisis. Relief is viewed as specialized and technically demanding work that is carried out during the occasional episodes of extreme disasters. This focus on episodic and extreme events hinders our seeing those who suffer the long term consequences of disasters and those most vulnerable to disasters, the exact groups the church is in the best position to care for. For example, in Haiti, cholera has taken 8,000 lives since 2010 and is a growing epidemic mainly impacting the rural poor, but the amount of aid to the country and the number of medical teams operating continue to be cut dramatically.

Misperception #2: Disaster work is mainly about caring for the immediate survivors.

This is a corollary of the above issue. Medically fragile people suffer for long afterwards as care is disrupted. Further, the more a community is socially vulnerable, the greater the damage from a disaster (Thomas, et al., 2013). The needs of this group become more apparent as the disaster response moves into longer term recovery, which is also when aid and public attention drop dramatically. Addressing vulnerability and long term recovery are best done by the local church where the church has a long term presence in the community and a continuing relationship with those in need. However, awareness of the need and

82

the importance of this role are compromised by the perception that the disaster is over once the destruction is cleaned up and repaired.

Misperception #3: Disaster work is better done by professional agencies.

We support church teams engaging in disaster recovery work, and do not see such work as a threat or concern. We do see a concern with the thinking that this is the sum of disaster ministry, a view that flows from focusing on extreme events. As we will see, there is a trend to teach churches specialized skills for disaster work, which can be useful, but can also imply that the core ministry of the church is insufficient for disaster related work. This does damage to the distinctive contribution by the church that is not in reaction to an extreme event, but flows from a clear sense of mission and consistent connection to the community.

This brings us to the central hypothesis of this paper: That disasters reveal the need to redeem community and creation by revealing the people who suffer from inequality, lack of care, injustice, and lack of access to resources. As such, disasters reveal the communities' basic need for the church as the body that gives agency to redemption. Therefore, disasters are not simply an opportunity for the church; they reveal the necessity for the work of the church. The work of the church is not primarily as specialists in disasters, but as the organization through which the redemption of the community and creation will be achieved.

Who Then Should the Church Work With?

If churches are to engage more extensively in serving their communities, with disasters serving as both an opportunity to serve and a measure of the community need to be served, then what shall be the church's relationship with other institutions in this work? This brings us to the second of our two categories of risk, the influence of state and non-governmental institutions.

The theory of institutional isomorphism asserts that institutions that work in related fields will come to resemble one another over time. This has been shown with non-governmental institutions and government agencies alike (Frumkin & Galaskiewicz, 2004). Burchardt (2013) documented this occurring in a large group of churches engaged in the campaign to halt the spread of HIV in South Africa. In this campaign, there was a decided shift in collaboration between church and NGO from NGOs recruiting volunteers via churches, to directly funding the churches to provide the program services. The campaign was quite successful, and likely more so than would have been possible without church participation in reaching local populations (Gunderson & Cochrane, 2012). However, this program had a clear impact upon the participating churches. Over time, the churches adopted structures and management practices that were encouraged by their NGO partners so that they would more efficiently and effectively manage the programs. Church ministries that were not aligned with the HIV campaign began to receive less support while HIV programming, in many cases, came to dominate the ministries of the participating churches. In one case, a church ceased to be recognized by the local community as a church, and instead was perceived to be an HIV service center.

The impact on the local church described by Burchardt took place in large part because a well-resourced organization (the Government and NGOs) was recruiting and influencing a poorly resourced organization (the church, especially poor and rural churches). This is a particular concern for rural and underdeveloped regions where it is often the case that churches and their staff cannot be fully supported from local resources. Under such conditions, receiving funding that provides employment for staff and allows them to focus on their church work can be a powerful inducement. This is a particular concern outside of the developed world, where churches are typically not able to pay their pastors or support them full time. This widespread poverty creates vulnerability (Englund, 2003). Further, once resources are provided to churches, they may find it difficult to sustain their work, especially when serving the poor and rural communities where there are insufficient local resources to maintain needed programs (Green, et al., 2002).

This disparity in resources is only one condition under which such influence can occur. Powell and Dimaggio (1991) describe the multiple conditions under which one institution will influence another, with the result of the two becoming more similar. These conditions include a more organized institution's influence over a less well organized one, and an institution with a more positive reputation for effectiveness or success having more influence over those with less of a reputation. As a result of these and other influences, simply by operating in the same field of endeavor (such as building community disaster resilience or recovery), it becomes more likely a group of institutions will move over time toward becoming more alike, and especially like the more powerful and respected.

Sometimes these influences are quite overt. For example, Hauck (2010) calls for actions to strengthen the management and leadership capabilities of churches so they can function as better partners with NGOs and be better equipped to help NGOs reach the local community. This seemingly helpful recommendation is made without considering the consequences for the church. It implies that the church is not sufficient as it is but must become more like an NGO to be effective in serving the community.

The church's ministry does not need to be at risk when it engages in the community. Beckert (2010) notes that organizations working together do not necessarily become more alike. Under some conditions, cooperating institutions can maintain their distinctiveness and become even more distinctive from their co-operating institutions. When an institution has clarity regarding its own purpose and mission and a distinctive role, engaging with other institutions can serve to sharpen this mission. Applied to the church, it means the church needs to be very clear about its mission, including exactly why it is engaged in disaster ministry. It means that church members must be clear about how their role is related to fulfilling the core mission of the church rather co-opting the mission of an NGO. For the church, this speaks to the need to have a distinctive mission and clear role relative to other organizations and relative to disasters. Green et al. (2002) recommends "churches come to a considered understanding of their desired role ... and communicate this to government [and, we would add, NGOs], entering into dialogue concerning relative roles and relationships." (p. 351).

This then brings us back to our central aim, that the twin distortions of focusing on extreme disaster events, and operating together with NGOs and government agencies when serving disaster recovery risks undermining the mission of the church. The solution to this is for the church to be the church, by which we mean that it carry out its core mission as salt, light and compassion. Further, that the church do so with clarity and an understanding of the distinctiveness and great importance of being the church. What then does it mean to be the church, and how is that carried out in practice? We offer several models, based on observations in the field, in which we see churches playing distinctive roles that point to the qualities of salt, light and compassion.

Models for Church-based Disaster Ministry

The Church as a Bridge to those in Need

The concept of a bridge means connecting two communities. In this regard, the church can serve as a bridge between the vulnerable and those with the resources and responsibility to serve the vulnerable. The church brings not only the special role of representative of the local community, but also the position of trust built up over time through consistent service and caring ministry. We have seen multiple examples around the world of how a church can act as a bridge.

The church can be a bridge to programs that serve the vulnerable, and which the vulnerable population lacks the skills to access (thus the church assists with skills and enables access), lacks the awareness, or lacks trust in the program provider.

The church can be a bridge to technical resources. In East Africa, drought is becoming an annual event where it was once a 10 or 20 year event. This is threatening local communities. The church can serve as a point of access, both to bring in those with skills and resources to address the problem, and also as a way to communicate out to the world where a community is not receiving attention and needs assistance.

Finally, and this is not an exhaustive list, the church can be the bridge between the external NGO and the community, serving as advocate for the community and the facilitator for the NGO. This is not as the NGO's agent, but as the advocate for the community and local community expert that can inform the NGO services.

What Disasters Teach the Church

The Church as a Resilient Community

As mentioned, communities are more resilient when a set of social strengths are in place, such as low barriers to information and other resources, justice, education, health, and more. As the salt of the earth, a church impacts community resilience. First, it adopts the characteristics of a resilient community be promoting community, justice, and access to resources within the church. Then, by becoming a community characterized by openness, equity, justice and service, the church impacts the community in several ways. First, members gain experience with what is meant by resilience, and carry this into their interactions with the rest of the community. Second, by breaking down barriers, the church can demonstrate the benefits to the entire community and counter pressures toward isolation and privilege.

The Church as a Healing Community

Physical, emotional and spiritual healing are areas where the church can make a special contribution and highlight its distinctiveness (Aten, et al., 2013; Boan, 2012; Boan, et al., 2012). People often seek out the church and pastors following disasters and trauma as part of their effort to make sense of the experience and resolve conflicts around meaning and the nature of God. Churches are in a special position to equip volunteers to speak to these issues and offer comfort to survivors.

Healing is also a long term process. As noted at the start, the world's attention span is very short when it comes to disasters. Churches, especially when serving the local community, are in a position to demonstrate faithfulness and caring by persevering over the long term to aid with recovery. This means adopting disaster care not as an emergency service, but as a way of life, done on a continuing basis for as long as the need exists.

In addition to healing at the individual level, healing also occurs at two other levels. A church is a healing community when it offers group and community sources for nurturing, support and comfort. Social activities, community events, and other community level activities also serve to provide healing to those in need by demonstrating that they are part of a community that cares.

87

Finally, churches also heal by teaching healing, compassion and comfort. This teaching occurs in several places, such as from the pulpit during worship services, in Sunday School, and in other institutional programs. These more formal pronouncements influence the meaning people make of their experience and are a source of comfort and healing that can be overlooked.

The Church as Community Monitor

In some cases, disasters reveal the need to take political action to address the failure of the state. Bonhoeffer spoke to this as the rare but important role of the church to confront government when it is failing in its role to maintain law and order and serve the community (Metaxas, 2011). This is not to be confused with the church becoming politically active. Bonhoeffer emphasizes the church remaining independent of the state but not uninvolved. The church becomes the ultimate advocate for the community when it observes the state failing in its responsibility and acts to restore the state to its proper role. In terms of disasters, we described how disasters reveal the character of the community. In extreme cases, this can reveal corruption, failure of policy, or failure of justice in caring for the vulnerable. In these cases it is proper for the church to become an activist in revealing and correcting these failures of the state.

Implications

In Japan, where there is not a long history of church engagement with the community, NGOs, or government, carving out a distinct role for the church can seem difficult. We described how this can be the result of thinking of disaster work as technical or specialized work, rather than seeing disaster work as fundamentally an extension of the compassionate relationship to the community. The church is capable of playing a powerful role in a disaster when it knows the community and serves faithfully and compassionately for the long term. This is not a new role, it is the core role the church is called to fulfill. This is the role being carried out in the tsunami area in the north, and which is distinctive from other services. The church does not need specialists to carry this out. It simply needs to be what it is called to be: salt, light and compassion.

We conclude our discussion with listing four important implications of this discussion for preparing church leaders. First, the theology of church engagement into the community is fundamental to training church leaders. In our opinion, this topic has been unnecessarily complicated by the concern with social gospel that is seen as somehow undermining evangelism. The fact that this issue persists in many parts of the world shows that there is a lack of clear and well developed theology education on this issue.

Leadership is the second essential topic. We described how a lack of clarity in mission and the failure to show members how the ministries of the church fulfill the mission makes the church vulnerable to influence from non-faith-based institutions. Preventing this is a task for leadership, and schools need to address this in preparing future leaders.

Serving the vulnerable is fundamental to the identity of the church, but it is another topic that is distorted by media and politics. In some countries, being poor is characterized as being dependent, unmotivated, or overindulged by government programs. This is a distortion of what it means to be poor, and further, a distortion of who is vulnerable. Many more people are vulnerable than is generally recognized, but acknowledging vulnerability and accepting assistance is equated with many negative images, thus interfering with ministry. In serving the poor and vulnerable, we need to educate future leaders about what it means to be poor and vulnerable.

Finally, leaders need to demonstrate to church members what it means to be an advocate, to be a healing community, to be the resilient community, and more fundamentally, to be salt and light. The mission of the church is not a matter of teaching concepts or theological positions, it is about actions. If the church is to fulfill its' role of being salt and light, it must take actions that are visible and penetrate the community. Leaders will need to be educated to show the way to do this.

A Case Example: the Philippines

On November 8, 2013 Typhoon Haiyan (known locally Typhoon Yolanda) made landfall in Eastern Samar Province of the Philippines. When it landed, it became the largest typhoon to make landfall, with sustained winds of 315 kph. By the time the typhoon exited over the West Philippine Sea an estimated 9 million people were impacted, 5,200 killed, and a quarter million homes destroyed. In response, the Philippine Council of Evangelical Churches began organizing to assist the churches impacted and also equip churches for survivor care. The initial proposal was to train disaster chaplains who would then provide care to adults and children, and also orient church leaders and members to provide emotional and spiritual care. Further discussions led to broadening this proposal to provide multiple models for engaging church leaders and members in ministry.

The rationale for expanding program starts with the potential for impact. If the focus is limited to disaster chaplains and emotional care helpers, then a minority of church members would be engaged. While 750 is a significant number, it represents only 2.5% of the 30,000 church members and leaders in the Philippine Council of Evangelical Churches. Alternatively, if there are multiple roles available for church leaders and members, and if those roles included recognition of how existing ministries can serve those impacted by the typhoon, then the opportunities for impacting those in need would expand dramatically, ideally engaging the majority of churches in this ministry. Further, the focus on survivors, while essential, overlooks the broader impact on the country and the fact that people not immediately suffering loss from the typhoon can still be impacted indirectly and the damage from the typhoon spreads across the country. Thus, in collaboration with the Philippine Council of Evangelical Churches, the proposed program added training and mentoring in the following types of programs:

- Strategies for informing existing ministries for disaster response, with an emphasis on recognition and care for the vulnerable;
- Advocacy for the vulnerable, including strategies for communicating the needs of the vulnerable and promoting distribution of resources to those in need;
- Monitoring corruption, especially monitoring for selective distribution of resources, lack of transparency, and lack of accountability;

- Serving as a bridge to resources by assessing the needs within a area of ministry and then connecting with external resources to service those in need;
- Collaboration and communication, with an emphasis on keeping other ministries informed of services and resources, making needs known, and promoting coordination;
- Providing support services, from supporting training for those serving as a relief staff, providing retreat and rest for relief workers, and making the needs of the relief staff known to others who can provide resources.

Taken together with disaster chaplain and emotional and spiritual care training, these programs provide an array of ministry types that create expanded opportunities for service without requiring people to change roles to helpers or chaplains. Most importantly, it emphasizes showing churches how their existing work can serve the needs of disaster survivors and broadly address the impacts of a disaster, without changing the church into a specialized disaster program.

At this time these programs and trainings are being prepared for implementation, and their impact and success will be measured and reported in the future. We will be assessing whether people use the training provided, whether training reduces the risk for burnout among volunteers, and how many churches actually engage in one or more of the range of models of ministry promoted in the training.

1) 2011 disaster survivors stuck in housing limbo, asahi, 9/11/2013 <http://recoveringtohoku. wordpress.com/tag/temporary-housing/>, (accessed on 12/17/2013)

References

Aten, J., Boan, D., Hosey, J., Topping, S., Graham, A. & Im, H. (2013). Building capacity for responding to disaster emotional and spiritual needs: A clergy, academic, and mental health partnership model (CAMP). Psychological Trauma: Theory, Research, Practice, and Policy, 5(6), 591–600. doi: 10.1037/a0030041

Beckect, J. (2010). Institutional Isomorphism Revisited: Convergence and Divergence in Institutional Change. *Sociological Theory*, 28 (2), 150–166.

Boan, D., Aten, J. & Devangna, G. (2012). Strategies for Disaster Recovery Capacity Assessment and Development for Faith-based Organizations. Presentation to the Illinois Public Health Association, Lisle, June.

Boan, D. (2012). Implementing a disaster ministry. Presentation to pastoral workshop in disaster ministry. Japan Evangelical Association, Ochanomizu, Japan, November.

Bonhoeffer, D (1949). *The Cost of Discipleship*. Macmillan: New York.

Burchardt, M. (2013). Faith-Based Humanitarianism: Organizational Change and Everyday Meanings in South Africa. *Sociology of Religion*, 74, 1, 30–55.

Carroll, J. (1978). The effect of imagining an event on expectations for the event: An interpretation in terms of the availability heuristic. *journal of Experimental Social Psychology*, 14, 1, 88–96.

Englund, H. (2003). Christian Independency and Global Membership: Pentecostal Extraversions in Malawi. *Journal of Religion in Africa*, 33 (1), 83–111.

Frumkin, P. & Galaskiewicz, J. (2004). Institutional Isomorphism and Public Sector Organizations. *Journal of Public Administration Research and Theory* 14 (3): 283–307. doi: 10.1093/jopart/muh028

Green, A., Shaw, J., Dimmock, F., & Conn, C. (2002). A shared mission? Changing relationships between government and church health services in Africa. *The International Journal of Health Planning and Management*, 17, 4, 333–353.

Gunderson, G., & Cochrane, J. R. (2012). *Religion and the health of the public: Shifting the paradigm*. New York: Palgrave Macmillan.

Hauck, V. A. (2010). The role of churches in creating social capital and improving governance in Papua New Guinea: Lessons for working in fragile situations. *Public Administration and Development*, 30, 1, 49–65.

Hearn, J. (2002). The 'Invisible' Ngo: US Evangelical Missions in Kenya. *Journal of Religion in Africa*, 32(1), 32–60. doi:10.1163/15700660260048465

Hefferan, T., & Fogarty, T. (2010). The Anthropology of Faith and Development: An Introduction. *Napa Bulletin*, 33, 1, 1–11.

Hoksbergen, R. N. E. M. (2000). The evangelical church and the development of neoliberal society: a study of the role of the evangelical church and its NGOs in Guatemala and Honduras. *Peace Research Abstracts*, 37, 4.

Klinenberg, E. (2002). *Heat Wave: A Social Autopsy of Disaster in Chicago*. Chicago: University of Chicago Press.

Kniss, F., & Todd, C. D. (1997). The Effect of Religious Orientation on International Relief and

Development Organizations. *Journal for the Scientific Study of Religion*, 36, 1, 93–103.

Leusenkamp, A. M. J. (2010). Religion, authority and their interplay in the shaping of antiretroviral treatment in western Uganda. *African Journal of Aids Research*, 9, 4, 419–427.

Metaxas, E. (2010). *Bonhoeffer: Pastor, Martyr, Prophet, Spy*. Nashville: Thomas Nelson.

Nawyn, S. (2006). Faith, Ethnicity, and Culture in Refugee Resettlement. *American Behavioral Scientist*, 49, 11, 1509–1527.

Pinker, S. (2011). *The Better Angels of Our Nature: Why Violence has Declined*. Penguin: New York.

Pawell, W. W. & DiMaggio, P. J. ed. (1991). *The new institutionalism in organizational analysis*, University of Chicago Press.

Ramanath, R. (2009). Limits to Institutional Isomorphism. *Nonprofit and Voluntary Sector Quarterly*, 38, 1, 51–76.

Thomas, D., Phillips, B., Lovecamp, W., & Fothergill, A. (2013). *Social Vulnerability to Disasters*. Boca Raton, FL: Taylor Francis Group.

Vincent, R., & Byrne, A. (2006). Enhancing learning in development partnerships. *Development in Practice*, 16, 5, 385–399.

Woolnough, B. E. (2011). Christian NGOs in Relief and Development: One of the Church's Arms for Holistic Mission. *Transformation*, 28, 3, 195–205.

Lecture 2

'Whose Feet Are You Washing?'
Raising Leaders in the Midst of Suffering

George Kalantzis

"But there is a danger in the solitary life…the first and paramount danger is that of self-pleasing."—St. Basil of Caesarea [*ca.* 330–379 C.E.], *Longer Responses* 7.3.26

Nowhere have I found a better description of the dangers of a solitary spiritual life or ecclesial isolation than the one offered by St. Basil, the bishop of Caesarea in Cappadocia, in the late-fourth century C.E.

I am a historical theologian. As such, the world makes sense to me not simply by looking at the present, theorizing about who we are today, but always in connection to the past. I think within the company of those who have come before us, and the present only makes sense to me as part of a much longer story that runs deep into the narrative of those who have been faithful to God in the past. As Christians we do indeed confess that we are people of the narrative of God.

So, as we gather together to think about the role of the Church amidst catastrophe and suffering, and to imagine the possibilities of working with and alongside our neighbors, or to think together about what it means to raise Christian leaders for the future, I want to tell you a story. It is one of the many stories that come from the early Church, and one that has affected greatly Christians throughout history. It is the story of St. Basil, the bishop of the city of Caesarea in Cappadocia, in modern day Turkey, in the mid-fourth century.

The Famine of 369 C.E. and Basil's Response

As a bishop of an influential city in a province at the borders of the Roman Empire, Basil had been accustomed to both wealth and poverty in the great cities of Cappadocia. The fourth century was a time of transition, and even though Christianity had been making quick inroads in the conscience of the people of the Empire for almost two generations, Christians were no more than a sizeable minority by the middle of the century. Among other benefits, the religious freedom Christians had enjoyed since the beginning of the fourth-century, when Constantine became emperor, allowed for a wave of men and women who chose to practice Christian piety in monastic communities scattered throughout the remote part of the Empire.

Some monks believed themselves to be superior to other Christians and set themselves apart from the rest of the Church. Others were more pious, Christians searching for spiritual fulfillment, a life of prayer, meditation, and study of Scripture away from the noise and (spiritual) pollution of the cities and villages. They were looking for a personal relationship with God in the solitary life.

While deeply supportive of the monastic quest for spirituality and a measured solitude, Basil became sharply critical of this kind of isolated life, which he saw as deeply individualistic and a distortion of the Christian message. In his *Long Rule*, one of the most famous and influential collections of treatises on monasticism, Basil rooted his vision of the Christian life and practice in the Scriptures and articulated a coherent spirituality based on the example of Christ. Basil warned against the danger of incurvation and self-pleasing in the isolated life, and called for the monks to be God's hands and feet in the world. He wanted them to live their faith to the full. His plea to his brothers and sisters is so beautiful, that I ask for your indulgence to quote him at length:

There are other dangers in the solitary life besides those we have already described. The first and greatest danger is that of self-pleasing. For if a man has no one to examine his actions, he will think that he has already achieved the perfect fulfillment of the commandments, and, since his conduct is never tested, he neither notices his shortcomings, nor perceives any progress which he may have made, for the very reason that he has deprived himself of all opportunity for fulfilling the commandments.

For how will he practice the virtue of *humility*, if there is no one to whom he may show himself humble? How will he show *pity*, if he is cut off from the society of others? Or how will he show *forbearance*, if there is no one to oppose his wishes? But if some one say that instruction in the Holy Scriptures is sufficient for right conduct, he is like one who learns how to weave, but never weaves anything, or is taught the smith's art, but never deigns to put into practice what he has learnt. To such a man the Apostle would say, '*Not the hearers of the law are just before God, but the doers of the law shall be justified*' (Rom 2:13). For we see that our Lord Himself, from his exceeding great kindness, did not rest content with words or precepts, but expressly set before us an example of humility in the perfection of His love. For indeed, *He girded Himself and washed His disciples feet* [(John 13:4–5)]. Whose feet will you wash? To whom will you be a servant? Among whom will you be the last of all, if you live alone by yourself? How can that *good and joyful thing, the dwelling together of the brethren*, which is likened by the Holy Spirit to the precious *ointment that ran down from the high-priest's head* [(Ps. 133:1–2)], be accomplished in the life of the solitary?

The dwelling together of the brethren [(Ps. 133:1)] is indeed a field for the contest of athletes, a noble path of progress, a continual training, and a constant meditation upon the commandments of the Lord. It has for its one aim and end the glory of God, according to the commandment of our Lord Jesus Christ, who says, '*Let your light so shine before men that they may see your good works, and glorify your Father which is in heaven.*' (Mt. 5:16).[1]

Basil was no mere theorist. He was a priest, a pastor, and bishop at work. Basil insisted that, as Christians, we love our neighbor because it is in our nature as created by God.[2] Such love is natural. Basil understood that what others may aspire to—and even achieve—that is, goodness, love, identification with the poor and the marginalized, is a *constitutive element* for the Christian. Basil did not see love of neighbor as a challenge to the fulfillment of the Christian life. He understood well what Jesus said to the young lawyer in Matthew 22:36–39: "Teacher, which is the first commandment of the Law?" And Jesus answers him, "You shall love the Lord your God with all your heart, and with all your soul, and with all your strength, and with all your mind. This is the first and great commandment. And a second is like it, you shall love your neighbor as yourself."[3] As Dermot Tredget notes, "these two evangelical commandments have their origin in the Law of Moses from Old Testament. It is the same Lord

96

who speaks in both. But, reminds Basil, the second commandment not only follows the first but [it also] completes it. In stressing love of neighbour, Basil is implicitly putting the Christian life into a community context."[4] The isolated life is alien to Christianity and a theological oxymoron. John 13:35 identifies love as the sign of the true disciple. In keeping the first commandment we keep the second and vice-versa.

Basil's plea to his brothers and sisters was tested most severely in the winter of 369, at the aftermath of the severe earthquake that shattered Cappadocia and brought almost four years of devastating famine to the region. Thousands died; many more were displaced, fell ill, and eventually lost hope. In the midst of the catastrophe, Basil used his great skills and resources as administrator to change the cities in his jurisdiction. Orthodoxy was not his only concern. The plight of the needy, sickness, disease, and poverty were prevalent. Basil encouraged care for the poor and needy and insisted that care of the marginalized was the primary evidence of God's presence. This understanding of the role of the Church prompted Basil to establish a neighborhood that contained a range of buildings for the care of the sick and for the distribution of surplus food to those in need. This neighborhood came to be known as the *Basileiados* (*i.e.* "the city of Basil") and became a refuge for many generations. Under Basil's leadership, the Church established hospitals for the poor and hospices for Christian pilgrims, as well as a series of what would be called "urban monasteries," whose task was to provide charity throughout the city. It was Basil and his monks who spearheaded a large-scale relief effort in Cappadocia in the aftermath of the famine.

In the funeral oration commemorating Basil's life, his friend and colleague Gregory of Nazianzus tells us how he "united the solitary and the community life" by founding cells for ascetics that were connected to one another and in such proximity to the surrounding communities so that the "contemplative spirit might not be cut off from society" but instead work together for the glory of God.[5] Likening his friend to Joseph who offered relief both to the starving of Egypt and to his family (Genesis 41ff), Gregory of Nazianzen says that "he [Basil] assembled in one place those afflicted by the famine, including some who had recovered a little from it, men and women, children, old men, the distressed of every age. He collected through contributions all kinds of food helpful for relieving famine. He set before them caldrons of pea soup and our salted meats, the sustenance of the poor. Then, imitating the ministry of Christ, who, girded with a towel, did not disdain to wash the feet of His disciples, and employing his servants or, rather, his fellow slaves and co-workers in this labor, he ministered to the bodies and the souls of the needy, combining marks of respect with the necessary refreshment, thus affording them relief in two ways."[6]

Basil led the monks in this choreography of communal practices in which the life of prayer was animated by their care for the poor. Basil was deeply interested in "practical religion, in developing a sense of social responsibility among Christians."[7] Basil insisted that absence of generosity is a major sin. He believed that the chief and visible social sign of Christian conversion, life, and perfection would not be simply spiritual but that it would also influence society deeply—even economically. His *Basileiados* became quickly a concrete expression of what Basil called, "Christ's polity"[8] a new city, "the storehouse of piety….[w]here sickness is endured with equanimity, calamity is a blessing, and sympathy is put to the test."[9]

Raising Leaders through Suffering beyond Walls: A Few Modest Suggestions

Basil had understood long ago what theologian Stanley Hauerwas has often repeated in our own time, namely that "the church does not *have* a social ethic, but rather the church is a social ethic." That is, the Church is not one more player in the cluttered marketplace of ideas of virtue and social ethics, vying to show how much better the Christian way of life, morality, or even spirituality is. The Church is not in a mode of competition with the world. Nor does God ask her to be. Rather, the Church is the manifestation of the new life that comes in Christ. Basil taught his monks that the *culmen perfectionis* (*i.e.* the height of perfection) of Christian spirituality is none other than the *culmen charitatis*, that is, the utmost exercise of charity. No one was exempt, not even the monks.

The only way the world may know who God is, is to look at those who claim to have a relationship with God, those who claim to have been born of God, and see the very character of God reflected in us. As Peter Leithart has argued, "The first and chief defense of the gospel, the first 'letter of commendation' not only for Paul but for Jesus, is not an argument but the life of the church conformed to Christ by the Spirit in service and suffering. A community of sinners whose corporate life resembles Christ—that is the Church's first apologetic. The very existence of such a city is our main 'argument.'"[10] Or as James K.A. Smith puts it: "The church doesn't *have* an apologetic; it *is* an apologetic."[11] When the world asks, "Is there a God?" God's first and only response is, "Look at my people, called by my name" (*cf.* Isaiah 42:10–43:28 *et passim*). Like Israel of old, the Church is God's declaratory statement to the world of who God is, of what hope is, of what life without fear looks like.

Love and kindness, acts of mercy and justice, are not optional for the Christian; they are the phenotypical expression of our genotype. The church needs today leaders who understand that to "Love your neighbor" (Mark 12:31, Matthew 22:39) is not an idiosyncratic peculiarity for the few, but rather it is a dominical command.

The church needs today leaders who understand that even though salvation might have been personal, it is never an individual experience. The story of Basil and his city teaches us that Christians always need leaders who are willing to call the Church to make manifest to the world what it means to shed the vestiges of optimism and live in hope instead.

Like the fourth century, we too, need leaders who will show the Church what it means to live in an economy of abundance, an economy of *manna*, where plenty and grace overflow, precisely because "they cannot repay you." Amidst the prevailing economy of this world, the economy of fear, of scarcity and anxiety, the maddening futility of self-preservation and self-interest is supplanted by the Lord's invitation to see ourselves as co-participants in Christ's giving of himself.

Even in the time of catastrophe and overwhelming need, Basil understood that the Christian ministry to the world is not simply *holistic*, but truly *wholistic*. *Holistic* ministry looks at the holes in the system, the needs that require our attention and seeks to address those. Christians, however, recognize that we are *whole* people, in need of *wholeness* of life, spirit, mind, and body. Unlike many of the Greek and Gnostic philosophies that dominated the religious arena of the early Church, and who promised an escape from this word and the sufferings of this existence, the *good news* of the Gospel was rooted in the radical message that God was redeeming the world and making all things new: "Behold, I make all things new" (Revelation 21:5).

There is another saying by Hauerwas that is very well known, and I want to leave you with this: At the end, "The truthfulness of our claims is judged by the kinds of communities it produces."

1) Basil, *Reg. Fus.* 7:34–36. The critical edition of the *Long Rule* is found in Anna Silvas, *The Asketikon of St Basil the Great*. Oxford Early Christian Studies (Oxford: Oxford University Press, 2005). Here I am using the translation by E. F. Morison, *St. Basil and His Rule: A Study in Early Monasticism* (London: H. Frowde, 1912), 43–44 because I find that his translation presents Basil's passionate plea in a richer language.

2) Anthony Meredith S.J., *The Cappadocians* (London: Geoffrey Chapman, 1995), 29.

3) Matthew 22:36–39.

4) Dermot Tredget, OSM, *"Basil of Caesarea and His Influence on Monastic Mission"* (2005, http://www.benedictines.org.uk/theology/2005/tredget.pdf)

5) Gregory of Nazianzus, *Oratio* 43.62 (SC 384:260; trans. NPNF 7:415–416).

6) Gregory of Nazianzen, *Oration* 43.35. In Leo P. McCauley, *et al., The Fathers of the Church, vol 22: St. Gregory Nazianzen and Saint Ambrose: Funeral Orations* (Washington, DC: The Catholic University of America Press, 1953), 57–58.

7) Philip Rousseau, *Basil of Caesarea* (Los Angeles, CA: University of California Press, 1994), 136.

8) GNaz, *Oration* 43.63.

9) GNaz, *Oration* 43.63.

10) Peter J. Leithart, *Against Christianity* (Moscow, ID: Canon, 2003), 99–100.

11) James K. A. Smith, *Whose Afraid of Postmodernism* (Grand Rapids, MI: Baker Academic, 2006), 29.

Part II

Christian Forum for Reconciliation in Northeast Asia:
A New Community of Friendship

Brian Byrd

How can the people of Northeast Asia find the path to true reconciliation? Problems of history and understanding of history, social and economic inequalities, political ideologies, and religion plague this region. Disputes over boundaries appear intractable, as nations expand their military budgets in a climate of greed, fear, and anxiety.

The second section of this book reports and reflects on the Christian Forum for Reconciliation in Northeast Asia, a week-long gathering of theologians, pastors, and other Christian leaders and activists from Japan, Korea, China, Hong Kong, and the United States held in Nagasaki in April 2015.[1] The Duke University Divinity School Center for Reconciliation (North Carolina, USA) is the sponsor of this forum and similar ones in Korea (2014) and Hong Kong (2016). A scripture guides the Center and provides focus for the forums:

Therefore, if anyone is in Christ, he is a new creation; old things have passed away; behold, all things have become new. Now all things are of God, who has reconciled us to Himself through Jesus Christ, and has given us the ministry of reconciliation. (2 Corinthians 5:17–18, NKJV)

God, the Great Reconciler, calls us to be reconcilers in a world of broken relationships, to tear down walls of mistrust and misunderstanding that isolate, to build a new community of friendship.

Forums share a common approach and vision:
1. Participants come from a wide variety of backgrounds. All are actively involved in the midst of challenging and sometimes pain-filled situations in

the ministry of reconciliation. Each comes as an equal to the forum.

2. Forums provide fresh, creative space to help participants to discern a "New We" community.

3. Participants share vital time of worship, meals, and conversation for six days. This allows the fifty or so participants opportunity to get to know each other personally.

4. The forum schedule, strategically designed to foster such connections, flows as follows:

> Day 1: Knowing each other
>
> Day 2: The new creation: Reconciliation towards what?
>
> Day 3: Lament: Where are we and what is the story of where we are?
>
> Day 4: Hope: What does Christian hope for reconciliation and peace look like?
>
> Day 5: Spirituality for the long journey: How is God's ministry of reconciliation sustained over the long haul?

5. Forums emphasize sharing, the relativizing of problems, the confession of sin and the experience of forgiveness.

I. Nagasaki and Reconciliation

1. Welcome from the Archbishop of Nagasaki

Nagasaki provides a context rich in Christian history tragically familiar with yet not overcome by suffering. In this crossroads city, reconciliation has prevailed. Mitsuaki Takami, Archbishop of Nagasaki, welcomed the forum participants to his "deeply significant" parish.[2] Acknowledging the bitter feelings that still remain between Japan and the countries Japan invaded, the nuclear weapons that continue to threaten humanity, and the shadow of terror hanging over many lands, the Archbishop urged the participants to "cast into the turbulent waters of our world a stone that sends out ripples of peace."

Takami called for "humble reflection by the perpetrators of violence" as the first step toward true reconciliation. Taking the lead, he confessed his own nation's responsibility for the Fifteen Year War (1931–1945) which "mercilessly stole tens of millions of Asian lives." The words of Dr. Takashi Nagai (1908–

104

1951), Nagasaki's prominent scientist, poet, atomic bomb survivor, and fellow Catholic, sunk in:

> It is not the atomic bomb that gouged this huge hole in the Urakami Basin. We dug it ourselves to the rhythm of military marches. Who turned the beautiful city of Nagasaki into a heap of ashes?....We did. We started the foolish war ourselves. Who turned this bustling city into a huge crematorium and cemetery?...We did. We let the words "the one who lives by the sword will perish by the sword" go through one ear and out of the other. It is we the people who busily made warships and torpedoes.[3]

Nagai's life and writing reached across the sea that divides Japan and Korea to change the life of the former Archbishop of Daegu, the Most Reverend Paul Ri. Forced as a child to learn the language of the Japanese occupiers, Ri harbored long bitterness towards the Japanese. Discovering Nagai turned Ri's thinking around: he started a Korean-Japanese bishops exchange and an exchange program for Korea and Japanese young people. Ri personifies the message of Pope John Paul II: "Nothing comes from merely accusing each other. We must overcome the temptation to refuse to call out to others, the temptation to exclude."[4]

2. Nuclear War or Mutual Forgiveness?

No conversation in Nagasaki could ignore the atomic bomb. Takami allowed no justification for its use. He shared the letter he received from an American Catholic priest who came to Nagasaki to apologize: "We are all brothers and sisters of the victims of nuclear weapons. We share their suffering from nuclear radiation...fighting the attitude in our hearts that would justify even the wanton, inhumane destruction of human life."

Takashi Nagai, however, reflected and pled from his personal sorrow as the radioactive dust settled. After doing all he could to rally and assist his fellow survivors, Nagai had returned to the rubble of his home to find the bones of his wife who had died as she lived, in prayer, a melted rosary clutched in her hands. He lamented

Nuclear war is not at all beautiful or interesting. It is the most disappointing, most brutal and complete form of destruction. Only ashes and bones remain; nothing touches the heart…"War is such folly! Nobody can win or lose in a war. There is only destruction. Humans were not born to fight! Peace! Peace forever! [5]

Nagai showed the way to peace with his plea, "Let us forgive each other … because no one is perfect. Let us love each other…because we are all lonely. Whether it be a fight, a struggle, or a war, all that remains afterward is regret." [6] Regrettably, seven decades later, Pope Francisco still could charge, "Humanity has learned nothing from the atomic bombs that fell on Hiroshima and Nagasaki." The vision of Francisco's predecessor, Pope John Paul II, remains our unceasing quest:

The pillars of true peace are justice and that form of love which is forgiveness…all human beings cherish the hope of being able to start again that true forgiveness brings. Society, too, is absolutely in need of forgiveness. Families, groups, societies, states and the international community itself need forgiveness to renew ties that have been sundered, go beyond sterile situations of mutual condemnation, and overcome the temptation to discriminate against others. [7]

Sharing the wisdom of his superiors, Takami encouraged participants to build a new community, to seek relations based on mutual forgiveness.

3. Nagasaki's Christian History

Takami summarized the history of the Catholic Church in Japan, and in Nagasaki in particular. Japanese of all social classes accepted the Christian faith that Francisco Xavier and his followers introduced beginning in 1549. The ruling authorities, however, saw Christianity as the seed of troubles. They saw the teaching that all people are equal before God and the help offered to the suffering and poor as creating a breeding ground for rebellion against their power. Japan feared that after the European countries sending missionaries had increased the number of believers, they would invade Japan. Hideyoshi

Toyotomi thus banned Christianity as an "evil belief," expelled foreign mission-aries, and in 1597, had twenty-six Christians marched from Kyoto to Nagasaki, where they were executed on crosses as a warning to others. To the Japanese Christians, however these martyrs-saints became powerful examples of faith and courage they sought to emulate.[8]

In its zeal to eradicate Christianity, the Tokugawa regime closed Japan to foreign intercourse for 260 years. Policies such as *fumi-e*, where suspected Christians were forced to tread on a picture of Mary and Jesus, and the *shūmon aratame*, or examination of religion, where each Japanese man had to appear once a year in a temple or before a magistrate and declare officially to which Buddhist sect he and his family belonged, drove the "Kirishitan" underground. The authorities offered monetary rewards to anyone informing on edict violators. Some Kirishitans became martyrs, while others, while outwardly pretending to be Buddhists, maintained and passed on their faith. The policies were ostensibly to "protect the national treasure of human lives from foreign enemies, and to provide for peace and prosperity." Takami, however, saw the Kirishitans as no threat at all: "They never held bitterness, hatred, or desire for revenge in their hearts; they only forgave."

II. Pilgrimage to Nagasaki

1. Oura Church and the Discovery of the Japanese Believers

Takami's history lesson readied forum participants for their "Pilgrimage to Nagasaki," a tour on the third day of the forum to sacred and historic sites in the city, each rimmed with pathos, and often with spiritual beauty as well. Oura Church, built by the French Foreign Mission Society in 1864 in commemoration of the twenty-six martyrs, faces Nishizaka Hill, where the crucifixions took place. On March 17, 1865, Japanese believers from nearby Urakami approached the French Father Petitjean at Oura Church. To confirm he truly belonged to the Church of their ancestors, these women asked Petitjean three questions: "Are you married?" (The Protestant pastor they had met earlier had failed this test.) "Are you sent from Rome?" and "Do you have a statue of Mary?" In the church, they saw and knelt before the answer to their third question. "Our hearts and

107

your heart are the same," they rejoiced. Petitjean passed the test, and came secretly to celebrate mass for the Kirishitans. Along the path leading up to the church, a bronze relief depicts the five women meeting Petitjean for the first time.

The year 2015 marked the one hundred and fiftieth anniversary of this "discovery of the Japanese believers," celebrated by the Catholic Church and the city of Nagasaki with some fanfare. This "discovery," however, had led to more suffering for the Kirishitans. When they started to express their hitherto concealed faith, the new Meiji government scattered 3400 of the Urakami believers throughout Japan. Six hundred died in exile, and only in 1873, under pressure from western countries, were the signs prohibiting Christianity taken down.

According to Takami,

"The exiled Kirishitans returned home with nothing to start their lives again. They made no protest against the Meiji government, nor did they seek any revenge. Instead, they sought God's forgiveness for having tread on the sacred pictures and having outwardly pretended to be Buddhists. They prayed not only for themselves, but for their brothers and sisters who, unable to bear up under torture, had given up their faith. They also begged forgiveness for the sins of the officials that had tortured them. Seeking to make atonement, they created a 'hill of the cross' and there offered up prayers."

As our small group of modern-day reconcilers moved on to the Site of the Martyrdom of the Twenty-six Saints of Japan, we sensed we tread on sacred ground.

2. Oka Masaharu Memorial Nagasaki Peace Museum

We lingered beyond the allotted time at most stops on our pilgrimage, the Oka Masaharu Memorial Nagasaki Peace Museum no exception. This small two story structure located on a side street cannot be found on tourist maps, yet it documents an overlooked reality: "The non-Japanese people victimized by Japan's war of invasion remain forgotten and unrecompensed...The irresponsibility of an aggressor that refuses to provide its victims with apologies or compensation is a betrayal of international trust."[9] The museum provides a chronology of Japanese aggression in Asia, with sections on Aggression and "Unification under the Emperor," Forcible Recruitment of Laborers, the "Rape of Nanjing," Korean Atomic Bomb Survivors, and Postwar Compensation for non-Japanese victims of Imperial Japan and the atomic bomb.

Yasunori Takazane, professor emeritus of Nagasaki University, met us at the entrance to the museum he directs. Even before seeing the exhibits, a number of us engaged him in a lively question and answer session. Takazane told us how the museum came to exist, speaking with deep respect for the man whose legacy he upholds.

Masaharu Oka (1918–1994), a Lutheran pastor, was a member of the Nagasaki City Council and a representative of the Association to Protect the Human Rights of Koreans Living in Japan.

"Long before Japan's role as a wartime aggressor became an issue in Japan, Oka relentlessly dug up the squalid secrets of Japan's mistreatment of Koreans, and its failure to compensate the Korean victims of the atomic bomb in Nagasaki. His work led to the dedication of a marker in the Nagasaki Atomic Bomb Memorial Park memorializing the Korean victims of the disaster. Early in the morning of August 9 each year, a memorial gathering is held to remember these victims."[10]

"Oka always stood on the side of the weak and oppressed, the victims of discrimination, and took action for them, fighting against a government that refused to admit responsibility." This vision inspired Oka's coworkers to create the museum. They started without land, building or funding, and supported entirely by private contributions, accepting no assistance from any corporations or government entities. Takazane (himself an atheist) saw the improbable project move to completion "as though guided by Oka from the other world."[11]

Takazane related to us facts sleuthed out and recorded by Oka. In the period of confusion following the end of the war, company officials altered the records kept on Koreans and Chinese laboring in the Nagasaki shipyards and munitions factories, eliminating evidence of wage discrimination.

Fuller Theological Seminary Professor Hak Joon Lee heard this with deep personal interest as his own family's past came into focus. Lee recalled how his grandfather had come from Korea to work in Japan in the early 1930's. His own father was raised in Japan and did not receive a proper education. The grandfather brought his family back to Korea after World War II, where he soon died of exhaustion. Lee's father then struggled greatly to care for his family.

Moved by the work of Oka and the mission of the museum, Lee and his wife, Jackie, decided to do what they could to help. They have shared the story of the museum with their pastor and with friends in leadership positions in Korea, encouraging visits to the museum. They are also making a multilingual homepage for the museum.

3. The Nagasaki Atomic Bomb Museum

We hurried on to the much larger, government funded and maintained Atomic Bomb Museum. Buses filled with junior high school students in their school uniforms stop at this stolid edifice, built near Ground Zero and devoted to a moment by moment replay of the fateful day, to the devastation and relief work that followed, and to a nuclear-free world. A replica of the bomb hangs from the ceiling; maps depict the concentric circles of destruction, photographs recall the physical horror of the event. Stepping down into the underground center of the museum, the weight of the moment presses heavily into the mind. We looked, lingered, pondered and left, grateful for the welcoming air and greenery of the adjoining Peace Park. Our group stood with the Peace Statue behind us as Professor Xi Lian, born in China and teaching at Duke, led in prayer.

No one questions the horror of the atomic bomb, a humanitarian disaster that must never be repeated. The museum, however, does not explore all the ramifications of that day. What prompted Japan's emperor to surrender brought liberation, even life to many, including a member of our group. Professor Peter Lau, a pastor now teaching at Chicago's Trinity Evangelical Divinity School, shared the following personal story during morning worship.

On August 15, 1945, young Korean conscripts gathered at the railway station in Pyongyang, Korea, then a part of the Empire of Japan. Russia had entered the war on the side of the Allies and against Japan on August 8. These young men would ship off to Manchuria with the suicidal task of slowing the advance of the overwhelmingly superior Russian army. Having bid loved ones farewell, they would fight to the death in the name of the Emperor of Japan.

Christian Forum for Reconciliation in Northeast Asia

They could not expect to return. As they waited at the station, a high-pitched voice came quavering over the radio speakers. Emperor Hirohito was telling his subjects that the war was over. Japan had surrendered. Peter Lau's father was one of the conscripts at the Pyongyang Station on that day, in route to certain death. Spared by Japan's surrender, he lived to see his son immigrate to America. Korea and other Asian countries remember Japan's defeat as their Liberation Day.

4. Nagai Takashi Memorial Museum and Urakami Cathedral

Tour buses stop at the museum commemorating Dr. Nagai, but rarely for more than a five minute rush past the memoirs of Nagasaki's "First Honorary Citizen." Nagai's grandson, who directs the museum, gave a short talk, encouraging us to live wholeheartedly for others in our own circumstances. He denied there being anything extraordinary about himself—or his grandfather. Within the Catholic faith that he embraced in 1934, however, Nagai has been designated "Servant of God," the first step on the way to canonization. His life, a model of reconciliation, puts into sharp relief the dark valley of Showa imperialism and the atomic destruction and spiritual recovery of Nagasaki, and epitomizes the depth, beauty, and resiliency of the city's Christian community.

Nagai studied at Nagasaki Medical College, confident in the progress of science and the success of Japan. Like many young men of his time, he sought relief from hard study in the pleasure quarters. As his mother was dying, however, her gaze into his eyes told him there was a soul. This shook his materialistic worldview and set him on an earnest search for spiritual reality. He boarded in the home of a family that had been leaders of the underground Christians in the Edo period. There, he became strongly attracted to the daughter, Midori, and the purity of her faith. Japan invaded Manchuria, and Nagai was sent there in 1933 as a military doctor. He returned disillusioned with Japan's military and fatigued by war's cruelty.

Disembarking, he stood on the wharf and looked up at "the two Nagasakis....One is the Nagasaki of carnal love, and you can find it down in suburbs....places of the night dedicated to loose women, sake, and fun....the other city, the Nagasaki of Mary, [is] also a place of love, but a love sustained by prayer, sacrifice, and service. You can discover this second Nagasaki in the

Urakami Cathedral, on the Hill of the Twenty-six Martyrs, in the Oura pilgrim shrine, and in the monastery built by Maximilian Kolbe."[12]

At this crossroad, Nagai chose true love. He read the Bible and Pascal, knowing "the heart has reasons that reason cannot know." Sympathetic counsel from priests and poor lay believers alike soothed his aching heart. Guided and guarded by Midori's constant prayers, Nagai came to faith in 1934 and married Midori. In 1937, he returned to the war front in China, where sustained by his faith, he selflessly served the wounded on both sides. He returned home in 1940 and continued his work as a pioneer in radiology. This exposed him to massive doses of radiation, until in 1944, he was found to have leukemia and given three years to live.

In the atomic blast that took his wife, church, and most of the community, Nagai suffered injury and lost much blood. Still, he led relief efforts, for one month caring for the wounded until he collapsed and went into a coma. Nagai then heard a voice telling him ask Father Kolbe, whom he had known well in Nagasaki, to pray for him. Unknown to Nagai, Kolbe had volunteered to take the place of a condemned man in Auschwitz and been executed in 1941. Miraculously, Nagai recovered from the point of death.

On November 23, 1945, the priests at Urakami Cathedral asked Nagai to speak at the funeral for the 8,000 parishoners out of a Catholic community of 12,000 killed by the atomic bomb. Grieving the loss of his beloved Midori, Nagai told the mourners "it was the providence of God that carried the bomb to its destination." Nagasaki had not been the bomb's first target. He reasoned

"Is there not a profound relationship between the destruction of Nagasaki and the end of the war? Nagasaki, the only holy place in all Japan—was it not chosen as a victim, a pure lamb, to be slaughtered and burned on the altar of sacrifice to expiate the sins committed by humanity in the Second World War?...we have forgotten that we are children of God; we have believed in idols; we have disobeyed the law of love...in order to restore peace to the world it was not sufficient to repent. We had to obtain God's pardon through the offering of a great sacrifice." Our church of Nagasaki kept the faith during four hundred years of persecution when religion was proscribed and the blood of martyrs flowed freely. During the war this church never ceased to pray day and night for a lasting peace. Was it not, then, the one unblemished

Christian Forum for Reconciliation in Northeast Asia

lamb that had to be offered on the altar of God? Thanks to the sacrifice of this lamb many millions who would otherwise have fallen victim to the ravages of war have been saved. We Japanese, a vanquished people, must now walk along a path that is full of pain and suffering...But this painful path along which we walk carrying our burden, is it not also the path of hope, which gives to us sinners an opportunity to expiate our sins?...We must walk this way of expiation faithfully and sincerely. And as we walk...let us remember how Jesus Christ carried His cross to the hill of Calvary. He will give us courage...Let us give thanks that Nagasaki was chosen for the sacrifice. Let us give thanks that through this sacrifice peace was given to the world and freedom of religion to Japan.[13]

Nagai angered some of the mourners with this understanding, but the years that followed only confirmed its truth in his heart.[14] Faithful to his wounded community, he chose to remain in Urakami, first in a flimsy hut built on the site of his former dwelling. In 1948, friends built to his specifications a new six-foot by six-foot hut he named Nyokodo, meaning "as yourself" house, from Jesus' command to "love your neighbor as yourself." There Nagai convalesced, prayed, and welcomed a steady stream of visitors, including Helen Keller and the Showa Emperor. Often working through the night, he wrote twenty books before finally succumbing to leukemia in 1951. Nagai used an honorarium from his writing to have one thousand cherry trees planted in Urakami in 1948, symbols of hope in the atomic wasteland. Most trees have been replaced, and their blossoms still grace the neighborhood.[15]

A visit to Urakami Cathedral concluded our pilgrimage. It had stood as the largest church in Asia before being destroyed by the bomb. After the war, the community began to rebuild in the ruins as its first priority a smaller place of worship that soon overlooked the bleak landscape, a symbol of permanence and hope. The cathedral itself, rebuilt in 1959, has kept scarred statues and broken brickwork, mute testimony to the nuclear whirlwind that swept all else away.

We sat in the smaller side chapel and listened to the lay guide's now familiar stories of her community's faith, suffering, and resilience. Emotionally drained from the day, our prayer mourned with tears the tragedies we had come closer to and claimed the promise of Jesus not to leave us, or any, as orphans.

Sue Park-Hur, a Korean-American pastor from Los Angeles, led worship the next day. She asked the Christians from Japan to come to the center of the room, and the other participants to lay hands on them and pray. All had come to know Japan more clearly now, and perhaps to see the land in a different light: Japan was no longer simply the unrepentant former imperialistic belligerent, but the land where twenty-six martyrs shed their blood, where faithful Christians had suffered relentless persecution, where atomic bombs had wrought unthinkable destruction, and where the fragile one percent population of believers struggles to survive, serve one another and the society, and rejoice in vibrant community. Twenty of us living and working in Japan knelt down and received the fervent prayers and blessings of our brothers and sisters from Northeast Asia and the United States. This touched many as the highlight of the week.

III. International Peace Symposium

1. Broken Walls

On the Sunday after the forum, some of the participants remained for an International Peace Symposium open to the public. Speaking in the hall adjoining the Nuclear Bomb Museum, Richard Hays, Professor of New Testament and Dean of Duke University Divinity School, presented the biblical vision for reconciliation. He told the story of the Catholic chaplain who blessed the flight that dropped the atomic bomb, only to wander through the rubble of Nagasaki days later, where he picked up a censer from the obliterated Urakami Cathedral. Hays' life theme rang clear: "The community of Jesus' disciples is called to be a light for the world. By obeying Jesus' radical teaching about nonviolence and peacemaking, they will...prefigure the peaceable kingdom God in a world wracked by violence." He insisted "peacemaking and nonviolent reconciliation are not optional political preferences; rather, they stand at the heart of the gospel and anchor the identity of the church."

For Hays, the biblical witness is clear: "Jesus' followers are called to be a community free of anger, lust, falsehood, and violence...the most startling and salient feature of this new model polis is the transcendence of violence through loving the enemy." Peacemaking is "constructive work...Jesus' rejection of violence models the community of discipleship he seeks to create, a community grounded in love and seeking reconciliation with enemies."

Hays paused where the Greek text in 2 Corinthians 5:17 "blurts out" that we are "New Creation," redefining our humanity and setting us out on a mission, "literally, 'placing in us the word of reconciliation.'" We "embody" reconciliation. Hays insists the cross and resurrection do not "prepare our souls for a disembodied future life in heaven," but "rather...tear down the wall of hostility between us violent human beings."

2. Reconciled Reconcilers

Forum Director Chris Rice, the son of missionary parents, spent his formative years in Korea, where he grew up hearing stories of Japanese aggression. Even as he returned to the United States and then dedicated his life to the mission of reconciliation, he harbored bitterness towards the Japanese. Rice lived for many years in a Christian community that brought together blacks and whites (John Perkins' Voice of Calvary), started another community, and wrote books on his experience. Duke University then called him to establish the Center for Reconciliation.

The Center's first reconciliation initiative brought together Christian leaders from the war torn East African Lakes nations. Rice's thoughts then returned to Northeast Asia and his South Korean roots. In planning the current forum, he invited three Japanese Christian leaders to participate in an introductory session at Duke, along with leaders from Northeast Asia and the United States. Although the time of shared fellowship, worship, and preparation went well, at mealtimes in the cafeteria he found himself avoiding Pastor Katsuki Hirano, senior member and spokesperson for the Japanese contingent. Not until Chris visited Japan and spent time with Hirano in Nagasaki working out the details for the forum, enjoying relaxed conversation and interaction, did the wall of ice in his heart begin to melt away, unable to withstand the warmth of life shared in Christian ministry. As the public symposium in Nagasaki came to a close, Rice shared this personal journey towards reconciliation, Hirano at his side.

IV. Conclusions

1. The Pride and Paradox of Nagasaki

Nagasaki takes pride in its identity. A brochure touts the Precious Identity (Pride) of Nagasaki, announcing its candidacy for recognition as a World Heritage Site. The top half of the cover page has a statue of Mary holding the Christ Child. The bottom half has a picture of Hajiima, or Battleship Island (*Gunkanjima*), site of an abandoned coal mining city symbolizing Japan's industrial revolution that began with the Meiji Era (1868–1912). The cover exudes "Memories link us with the past. Hope links us with the future. World Heritage Sites that show not only material things, but the heart."

Today, Battleship Island tours take visitors back in time to recall a model of community, ingenuity, efficiency, and self-sacrificing contribution to the making of modern Japan. Duke Professor Xi Lian, however, calls the island a site, by our standards, of industrial slavery. The Oka Museum documents the dark reality of Japanese and Korean workers facing torture or death if caught trying to escape.

Takami sees the once persecuted churches now celebrated as relics of the Catholic presence in the city as "a sign of the times." He urges "work so that Christianity is rightly understood, and can give even some small positive influence to society." Ultimately, he states, "Christ the Lord himself is our peace."[17] Yet in this world, peace is not just a gift. Takami charged "To rebuild peace that has been destroyed, we perhaps need to make even more efforts." The forum took a small step in this direction.

2. The Future of the Christian Churches in Nagasaki

Christian peace and reconciliation need a constituency. This raises the question: How fares Christianity in Nagasaki today? Who will carry on the torch of the martyrs? Will the churches thrive as vital places of worship and community, or become mere museums, like many of their counterparts in Europe?

Nagasaki stands at a crossroads, not only geographically, but in time. Visiting the city gave me some opportunity to take its Christian pulse. Our forum met at the Yasuragi ("peaceful rest") Iojima Hotel, a forty-five minute drive from Nagasaki City. Half of the residents on the small, hilly island are Catholics. For two of our morning worship times, we borrowed nearby Saint Michael's Church, set on the hillside overlooking Nagasaki Bay. The Catholic sister pointed out buildings nestled higher up the steep slope. "That used to be a nursery school. When we no longer had any children coming, we made it into a home for the elderly."

The other church on the island antedates St. Michael's, but has been rebuilt. A series of steps wind between houses and gardens perched on the hillside to the church. Two women had opened the church to arrange the flowers for Sunday mass. We learned that at most twenty people come, some picked up and driven to church by the new priest who has responsibility for the island's two churches. The women preparing the flowers, both over sixty, spoke of themselves as the young members of the congregation.

Back at the hotel, a worker at the front desk escorted me to the free laundry machines. "I am a Christian," she shared enthusiastically, pointing to her cross as we walked. "My Christian name is Maria." The cheerful twenty-four year old attends the local Catholic Church. I asked if there were other Christians working at Yasuragi Hotel, but she said she was the only one.

On our last Sunday in Nagasaki, some participants worshipped at Urakami Cathedral. Parishioners of all ages but averaging well over sixty filled to about thirty percent capacity the huge sanctuary. The young priest had just been called from his hillside parish where cars could not go, yet the aging believers still dragged themselves to church, to serve at Urakami. He spoke from John 10:11, "The Good Shepherd lays down his life for the sheep." To know each other as a shepherd knows his sheep is the starting point for solutions to our problems. We must make our talks "friendly" and close the gap with inactive members. The priest spoke in familiar terms. Referring to the Japanese virtue of hospitality (*motenashi*), a selling point in Tokyo's bid for the 2020 Olympics, he vowed to set the example in reaching out to people who no longer came to church. He related a touching scene from a TV drama: A man wanting to observe the memorial of his wife's death came alone to a restaurant. The waiter, who had just lost his father, shed tears at man's story of his wife. The priest envisioned a church where those once strangers could come to share joys and sorrows. We pray for his success, the church's survival, and revival in Japan.

3. "The Sky Over Nagasaki"

1. *The sky over Nagasaki stretches out from our feet, the blue sky watching over the way of the martyrs, calling back to our memories this time of loss, as I stand at the crossroads of heaven and earth.*
2. *The sky over Nagasaki shrouded in black night, stained with the ashes of those blasted by the bomb, weeping for this time of loss, as I stand at the crossroads of heaven and earth.*
3. *The sky over Nagasaki invites us to the kingdom of God, embracing the faith of the people of earth, as I stand at the crossroads of heaven and earth.*
   Seeking a new time, I am here to meet Jesus, who joins heaven with earth.

A combined choir from the city's Protestant churches sang this stirring hymn for the International Peace Symposium.[17] In our week together in Nagasaki, we too had remembered the blood of the martyrs, wept for the black night of the holocaust, and stood at the crossroads of heaven and earth, all the while sharing precious fellowship in the presence of Jesus. Encouraged, shaken, and challenged, we then continued on our own pilgrimages, looking more deeply at the difficulties of history, seeing more clearly our common humanity, each seeking again where we are called to send out ripples of peace, longing to experience and extend to others the joy of the reconciled community.

1) Dedicated to fellow participant Richard Hays, my professor at Yale Divinity School (1981–1983) and guitar strumming fellowship leader, who with his wife Judy opened their home as a place of worship, Bible study, storytelling, and reconciliation, prefiguring this forum.
2) The bishop's roots lie deep in the local Christian community. In the sixteenth century, his ancestor had been sent to Europe as a member of a Japanese Christian delegation.
3) *A Hill in Bloom* (1949). Quoted by Takami.
4) Message of His Holiness Pope John Paul II for the Celebration of the World Day of Peace, January 1, 2002, "No Peace Without Justice, No Justice Without Forgiveness," Nos. 2. 8. 9. Quoted by Takami.

5) *A Hill in Bloom*.

6) From *Peace Tower* (1949).

7) "No Peace Without Justice."

8) From Takami's welcome message, translated and edited by the author.

9) From the pamphlet that introduces the museum in Japanese, English, Korean, and Chinese.

10) From Takazane's October 1995 eulogy of Oka.

11) Ibid.

12) Quoted by Paul Glynn in *A Song for Nagasaki: The Story of Takashi Nagai—Scientist, Convert, and Survivor of the Atomic Bomb*. Ignatius Press, San Francisco 2009, pp.100–101.

13) From *The Bells of Nagasaki* by Takashi Nagai, Kodansha International, 1984, pp.106–110.

14) "Hiroshima met with the same fate as Nagasaki, yet witnesses to the annual memorial occasions note the different spirit that marks each city: "*Sakebi no Hiroshima*, inori *no Nagasaki*" ("Shouting Hiroshima, praying Nagasaki.") Outsiders come to Hiroshima to make a political statement, while "Nagasaki seems to have has accepted its destiny as a 'whole burnt offering' (holocaust) that brought the war's end to Japan and peace to the world." "Nagai, more than any other individual, is responsible for the very spiritual atmosphere in Nagasaki's commemoration of the A-bomb." (*A Song for Nagasaki*, pp.257–261.

15) "All That Remains," a recent movie on Nagai's life takes its title from the scripture, "the grass withers, the flower fades, but the word of the Lord remains forever" (Isaiah 40:8) that impressed and comforted Nagai amidst the atomic devastation.

16) Ephesians 2:14–16; Colossians 1:20.

17) *Nagasaki no sora wa*, by Nozomi John Kato; translation by Byrd.

Contributors

About the Authors

Atsuyoshi Fujiwara

Fujiwara is Professor and University Chaplain at Aoyama Gakuin University. He has also taught at Tokyo Christian University, Seigakuin University, and Keio University. He received a PhD from Durham University in England.

Fujiwara is the founding pastor of Covenant of Grace Church, Japan Baptist Convention, in downtown Tokyo. He is active in academic research, church ministries, and ecumenical dialogues, and he chairs the International Theological Symposium Committee on Post-disaster Japan and Christianity.

Fujiwara's recent writings include: Theology of Culture in a Japanese Context: A Believers' Church Perspective (Princeton Theological Monograph Series, Pickwick Publications), "Christianity and War," and "Why we need the Church in Japan."

Brian Byrd

Byrd has been a member of the Seigakuin University Research Institute since 2003. He graduated from Yale Divinity School in 1984, and came to Japan that year as a missionary. He wrote his PhD dissertation, *Toyohiko Kagawa: A Sympathetic and Critical Study of a Japanese Christian Leader*, at Seigakuin University (2012). Throughout his career he has worked in English education for children, making numerous presentations and publishing books and papers. He also teaches English Bible classes.

Juan Martínez

Martínez, PhD, is Associate Provost for Diversity and International Programs, the Academic Director of the Hispanic Center, and Professor of Hispanic Studies and Pastoral Leadership at Fuller Theological Seminary in Pasadena, California.

He is an ordained Mennonite Brethren pastor. He has worked as a church planter, director of a Bible Institute, and rector of a seminary in Guatemala. His academic work focuses on Latino Protestantism in the United States. His writings include *Los Protestantes Latino—Protestantism in the United States and Churches, Cultures & Leadership—A Practical Theology of Congregations and Ethnicities.* Martínez visited Tohoku in 2012 during his trip to Japan to lecture for the first post-disaster symposium.

Yoshito Inamatsu

Inamatsu studied social welfare at Kwansei Gakuin University and began working from 1979 at Kohitsujigakuen (Lambs' School), an institution for children with severe mental disabilities. He became chair of Kohitsujigakuen in 1995. Seeking to run the institution aware of local networks and questioning the new practices of social welfare, he continues to experiment, learning through trial and error. He is currently a member of Ensyu Eiko (Glory) Church of the United Church of Christ in Japan (UCCJ). He has served since 2005 as chair of the Japan Christian Social Work League. From 2011 to 2013, he worked in the UCCJ's Great East Japan Earthquake Disaster Response Headquarters. He has served as a lay member of the UCCJ National Committee since 2012.

Isao Kikuchi

Kikuchi is Bishop of Niigata Diocese and President of Caritas Asia and Caritas Japan. Born in Miyako, Iwate, he graduated from Nanzan Graduate School of Theology in 1986 and was ordained as a priest of the Divine Word Missionaries (SVD). He worked in parish ministry in Ghana, West Africa from 1986 to 1994, and in 1995 joined Caritas Japan as a volunteer for the Rwanda Refugee Camp in then-Zaire. He was a lecturer at Nanzan University from 1996 to 2004, appointed Bishop of Niigata in 2004, and took leadership of Caritas Japan in 2007 and Caritas Asia in 2011.

Masanori Kurasawa

Kurasawa was born in Nagano City, Japan, and studied theology and missiology at Tokyo Christian Theological Seminary and Fuller Theological Seminary. He has served as president of Tokyo Christian University (TCU), and is currently a professor of missiology at TCU and its graduate school, and directs the TCU

About the Authors

Faith and Culture Center. He is a board member of Japan Missiological Society and Japan International Food for the Hungry, president of the Japan Lausanne Committee, and a pastor at Shonan Christ Church in Kashiwa City (a member of the Japan Alliance Christ Church).

Michio Hamano

Hamano graduated from Sophia University in Tokyo (B.A. 1984, M.A. 1988) and Seinan Gakuin University in Fukuoka (B. Theology, 1992). He studied at Heidelberg University in Germany, and received a D. Min. degree at the Pacific School of Religion in Berkeley (2007). He pastored Nankodai Baptist Church (Sendai) in the Japan Baptist Convention and worked as a researcher and director of the Research and Training Institute for Missions of the Japan Baptist Convention. He is currently an associate professor in the Department of Theology at Seinan Gakuin University. His publications include What is Mission? (2012) and *Why We are Against the Protection of National Secrecy Law* (2014) (both coauthored).

Akira Fujikake

Fujikake graduated from Daito Bunka University Department of Literature in 1982 and has a PhD from Seigakuin University. He is licensed as a clinical psychologist. He spent the first part of his career working as a psychologist for the Ministry of Justice, serving finally at the Toyama Juvenile Detention Facility as chief specialist before moving on to university work. He is currently an associate professor at Seigakuin University. He serves on the boards of the Japanese Association of Clinical Drawings and the Japanese Association of Criminal Psychology.

He has written many books in Japanese including *Introduction to Counseling of Delinquents, Introduction to Art Testing and Therapy, Living Just the Way You Are, The Psychology of Rain, Four-forty in the Afternoon*. He coauthored *The World of the Bible, Murakami Haruki and the Soul, and Caring for the Heart of Disaster Victims and Relief Workers*.

Hajime Hori

Hori is pastor of Tsuruse Megumi Kirisuto Church and a part-time instructor at Seigakuin University. He is a certified clinical pastoral counselor. He works as a telephone counselor at the Seigakuin University General Research Institute Counseling Research Pastoral Counseling Center, teaches part-time at Lutheran Gakuin University, and manages the Japan Pastoral Counseling Association. He has been a board member for Tokyo Helpline (*Inochi No Denwa*) and King's Garden Saitama, and a Bible instructor for NHK Gakuen. His writings in Japanese include *Care for the Heart of Disaster Victims and their Supporters* (coauthored), *A Walk for the Heart, Space in the Heart for the Soul's Healing*, and *Evangelical Theology and Pastoring*.

Makoto Suzuki

Suzuki graduated from the Nihon University Department of Law. After working in a private company, he became a staff member for the American missionary organization Life Ministries (now Asian Access). He graduated from Seikei (Covenant) Seminary and pastored Gospel Christ Church, then Totsuka Megumi Church (Fukuin Dendo Kyodan). He has been Director of Education, Director of Evangelism, and a member of the steering committee for the denomination. He currently directs the Great East Japan Earthquake support group, Isaiah 58 Network.

Yukikazu Otomo

Otomo is senior pastor of Shiogama Bible Baptist Church (Japan Conservative Baptist Association). He also serves as director of Miyagi Mission Network, and as a board member of Japan International Food for the Hungry and Asian Access Japan. Otomo lost his uncle and the family home in Wakabayashi, Sendai in the March 11, 2011 tsunami disaster. He began relief activities one week later and soon after started "Hope Miyagi," a church-based project for helping others rebuild their lives. Otomo has a D.min. in Practical Theology from Luther Rice Seminary. He dissertation was entitled, "A Proposal for Church Multiplication in Miyagi Japan: A Laity - Based House Church Model" (2011).

Takashi Yoshida

Yoshida directed the Sendai Christian Alliance Disaster Relief Network "Touhoku Help" and pastored a Reformed Church in Sendai. He is now president of Kobe Reformed Seminary and pastor of the Koshien Reformed Church. His writings include *Calvin's Theology and Spirituality: Meditations on*

About the Authors

the Life to Come, and *The Future of Social Welfare and the Church* (in Japanese). He has translated works on the Heidelberg Confessions and Catechism and G. E. Ladd's *The New Testament and Higher Criticism.*

David Boan

Boan has a PhD from Biola University. He is an Associate Professor at the Wheaton University Department of Psychology, and directs the Humanitarian Disaster Institute (HDI) at Wheaton. Boan has more than 30 years of experience as a clinical psychologist, and works now to bring together the church and the local community, focusing his energies on developing programs to help the weak in society, such as the disabled and aging. He has developed programs to improve local community health services in the USA, and has developed guidelines for sustainable, high level support for developing countries. Boan serves as a disaster response project advisor for the World Evangelical Association (WEA).

George Kalantzis

Kalantzis received his M.A in Biblical Studies at Moody Graduate School, his Masters in Theological Studies at Garret Theological Seminary, and his PhD at Northwestern University. He is an Assistant Professor of Bible and Theology at Wheaton University, where he also serves as the first director of the Early Christianity Research Institute. Born in Greece, his research focuses on Christology and on the development of the doctrine of the Trinity in the Early Church. He seeks to link the church and the world, to build up the church to become the church that revolutionizes the world, and following Stanley Hauerwas's suggestion, "a community that develops the person."

His writings include *Caesar and the Lamb: Early Christian Attitudes on War and Military Service* and *Evangelicals and the Early Church: Recovery, Reform, Renewal.*

A Theology of Japan Monograph Series

Hideo Ohki, Atsuyoshi Fujiwara,
David Oki Ahearn, Tomoaki Fukai,
Woon-Hae Nag

A Theology of Japan:
Origins and Task in the
Age of Globalization
A Theology of Japan: Vol. 1

Softcover 232 × 183 121pp.
1200yen (without tax)
ISBN 978-4-915832-59-8 (2005)

This first volume of the monograph series, *A Theology of Japan*, explores a theology that arose in post-war Japan and moved out to Asia and the rest of the world. It also considers from a theological perspective the sixty years following the end of the war.

Special Issue from the Seigakuin
University International Symposium
Atsuyoshi Fujiwara ed.

Church and State in Japan
since World War II
A Theology of Japan: Vol. 2

Softcover 232 × 183 164pp.
2500yen (without tax)
ISBN 978-4-915832-65-9 (2006)

The symposiasts included Noriyoshi Tamaru (Professor Emeritus, Tokyo University) from Japan, F. W. Graf (Professor, Munich University) from Germany, and W. J. Everett (Professor Emeritus, Andover-Newton Theological Seminary) from the United States. This issue includes all of their presented papers as well as the responses to them.

Yasuo Furuya

History of Japan and
Christianity
A Theology of Japan: Vol. 3

Softcover 232 × 183 179pp.
2500yen (without tax)
ISBN 978-4-915832-68-0 (2006)

The history of Japan has been indirectly or directly influenced by Christianity more than may be apparent, as this volume so ably shows. The understanding presented here is indispensable for any theological inquiry into Japan, or "theology of Japan."

Atsuyoshi Fujiwara ed.

"A Theology of Japan"
and the Theology of
Hideo Ohki
A Theology of Japan: Vol. 4

Softcover 232 × 183 110pp.
2500yen (without tax)
ISBN 978-4-915832-84-0 (2009)

This volume contains Professor Hideo Ohki's writings on the project he initiated, "a theology of Japan." It also contains a response to "a theology of Japan" from the West by Dr. Alan Suggate.

Seigakuin University Press

1-1 Tosaki, Ageo, Saitama, Japan 362-8585
press@seigakuin-univ.ac.jp

A Theology of Japan Monograph Series

Tomoaki Fukai, Christoph Schwöbel, Alister McGrath, Yoshiaki Matsutani

Protestantism and Democracy
A Theology of Japan: Vol. 5

Softcover 232 × 183 119pp.
2500yen (without tax)
ISBN 978-4-915832-85-7 (2009)

This fifth volume contains selected essays from two conferences that Seigakuin University General Research Institute hosted in 2008, "Rethinking the Tradition of Liberal Democracy since World War II" and "Trinitarianism: Going Beyond Criticism from Monotheism and Radical Pluralism."

Atsuyoshi Fujiwara, Brian Byrd, eds.

Post-disaster Theology from Japan
How Can We Start Again?
Centurial Vision for Post-disaster Japan
A Theology of Japan: Vol. 6

Softcover 232 × 183 128pp.
2500yen (without tax)
ISBN 978-4-907113-00-1 (2013)

This volume presents for a wider audience the voices of theologians and church leaders who gathered in Tokyo to consider "How Can We Start Again? Centurial Vision for Post-disaster Japan" one year after Japan's March 2011 disaster at the First Great East Japan Earthquake International Theological Symposium.

Atsuyoshi Fujiwara, Brian Byrd, eds.

The Church Embracing the Sufferers, Moving Forward
Centurial Vision for Post-disaster Japan:
Ecumenical Voices
A Theology of Japan: Vol. 7

Softcover 232 × 183 134pp.
2500yen (without tax)
ISBN 978-4-907113-09-4 (2014)

The Church Embracing the Sufferers, Moving Forward continues the task of *A Theology of Japan: Vol. 6*. Following the keynote address by Fuller Seminary President Richard Mouw, voices from Japan reflect on and relate the experience of the church as it has dealt with the aftermath of the disaster and sought to take positive steps forward.

Yoshibumi Takahashi ed.

Reinhold Niebuhr, Christian Realism and Social Ethics
A Theology of Japan: Vol. 8

Softcover 232 × 183 114pp.
2500yen (without tax)
ISBN 978-4-907113-12-4 (2014)

This book includes the keynote speeches by professors Robin W. Lovin and Sun Bihn Yim with responses by Japanese scholars at the International Symposium, "Reinhold Niebuhr: His Religious, Social, and Political Thought" (June, 1913), and other lectures delivered by professor Lovin at International Christian University, Tokyo Union Theological Seminary, and Seigakuin University.

Seigakuin University Press

1-1 Tosaki, Ageo, Saitama, Japan 362-8585
press@seigakuin-univ.ac.jp